Around The Farm Gate

A Treasure Trove of
Stories From 50 Authors

Edited by PJ Cunningham

Ballpoint Press

Published in 2015 by Ballpoint Press
4 Wyndham Park, Bray, Co Wicklow, Republic of Ireland.
Telephone: 00353 86 821 7631
Email: ballpointpress1@gmail.com
Web: www.ballpointpress.ie

ISBN 978-0-9932892-5-5

Book design and production by Joe Coyle Media&Design,
joecoyledesign@gmail.com

Cover photography: © Irish Farmers Journal

Printed and bound by GraphyCems

Contents

Around The Farm Gate

'Irish Farmers Journal'

IRISH people have a great reputation for storytelling. Indeed some of our best loved writers have created characters that are so familiar we can instantly recognise them in our neighbours and friends.

But that story-telling gene isn't just the preserve of our greatest playwrights, it is something that is innate in so many Irish people and is alive and well in rural areas.

Take your place around any kitchen table and the ordinary becomes extraordinary. An oral history passed from generation to generation is there to be shared. Field names, farmyards, family histories and farming practice could keep conversations flowing deep into the night.

This book gives people the opportunity to share the stories of their place and people and how they went about their everyday lives. And their stories are like golden threads that link us to those who went before.

The *Farmers Journal* is delighted to collaborate with PJ Cunningham and *Countrywide* in producing this book and indeed most of the credit must go to the many, many people who took the time to share their stories. Enjoy the read and the memories.

Mairead Lavery
Editor, *Country Living* (*Irish Farmers Journal*)

RTÉ's 'Countrywide'

AROUND the Farm Gate is a colourful tapestry of unique memories and stories of life on the land in rural Ireland, a rich collection of events that happened but are seldom documented, until now. From threshing oats, driving cattle to the local fairs, thinning turnips or cocking hay, the experience of growing up in rural Ireland is awash with anecdotes and yarns focused mainly on life on the land.

Farming life was a tough existence but through a combination of a strong faith and an honest work ethic, families managed to keep the show on the road and much of that life shines through in this collection of stories from across the country.

PJ Cunningham, himself a son of the faithful Offaly soil, first collaborated with us to write a radio piece about his memories of growing up on a farm. From this spawned the idea to gather this collection of other similar memories. When he came to us with the idea of this book, I knew immediately it was an ingenious plan as evidenced by the avalanche of stories which, up until now, had been buried in the minds of ordinary people dotted up and down the country.

I want to thank our listeners for buying into this project with such enthusiasm and I am delighted that Countrywide and the Irish Farmers Journal have joined forces with Ballpoint Press to produce what is a delightful result. Happy reading.

Damien O'Reilly
Presenter, Countrywide, RTÉ Radio 1

Introduction

THE genesis of *Around The Farm Gate* came from the feedback I received from people who had read my own books, *The Lie Of The Land* and *The Long Acre*, which were published over the past few years.

Such was the depth and variety of tales, it struck me that if we didn't commit these stories to print, they could be lost forever.

I approached RTÉ and the *Irish Farmers Journal* to see if they would be interested in teaming up to ensure this project of compiling a book of such stories became a reality.

Both organisations embraced the concept by publicising the idea of a collection of stories through RTÉ's highly regarded *Countrywide* show and the *Journal*'s acclaimed *Country Living* section.

What followed was beyond our wildest expectations as hundreds of stories arrived from across the country. There was a rich tapestry of tale-telling which made the final task of selecting 50 stories a truly challenging process.

For their input, enthusiasm and direction right from the start of this onerous task to its conclusion, I am indebted to Ian Wilson, Producer of Radio 1's *Countrywide* and David Leydon, Commerical Director of the *Irish Farmers Journal*. Both showed a great empathy right through the project and this collection is the richer for their contributions.

I would also like to thank Damien O'Reilly, the popular presenter, who has made *Countrywide* a unique listening experience each Saturday morning.

The *Irish Farmers Journal* has bucked the trend in current reading habits by continuing to grow in print and online. This is due to the leadership of Editor and CEO, Justin McCarthy and Mairead Lavery, Editor of *Country Living* whose support for this venture is greatly appreciated.

I would also like to acknowledge the contribution of RTÉ's Laura Beatty in getting the project over the line and to Clodagh Carey and Ramona Farrelly from the *Irish Farmers Journal* for the editorial and photographic sourcing they undertook for this book.

I am indebted to Joe Coyle for the way his attractive designs bring the front and back covers and the pages of this work to life.

Clyde Delaney's cartoons added a touch of fun to the pages. He is a regular contributor to the Katherine O'Leary page of the *Irish Farmers Journal* and also contributes to the *Irish Daily Mail*, *Phoenix Magazine* and RTÉ.

I would like to offer a sincere thank you to the hundreds of people who took the trouble to write down their experiences but whose stories didn't make the final cut. We could have used as many more again except for the constraints of space.

Finally, congratulations to those whose contributions make up this collection. You have produced valuable snapshots of an Ireland that has largely vanished over recent decades. My wish is that your work will help to frame for the next generation how their forbears lived their lives around the farm gate.

PJ Cunningham
Ballpoint Press

1 The Bend At The Church

Tom Rowley

THE turf sods in the fire were creeping red, grey ash from dying embers pushing out into a mottled pile on the hearth. It was 1960 and I was six years old, still in short pants and sitting on my father's knee beside the fire in Paddy Moran's pub at the bottom of the town in Castlebar.

The heat was burning irregular ABC patterns along my bare legs. My father was holding me, the youngest, close to him. His face snuggled up to mine. All I felt was a burning sensation, as if for a few seconds my soft young cheek was on fire.

He had travelled overnight on the ferry from Holyhead and then spent five hours on the train from Dublin to Mayo. He didn't realise that by then a brush from his stubble was like having sandpaper swiped across my cheek. I remember feeling the tears coming and tugging to pull away from him, afraid he would do it again. But he just held me tighter, wanting to be close.

At that age I didn't know that much about Tom, my father. He would come home twice a year for two weeks, in the summer and at Christmas, and so he was like a stranger who dropped in now and again. My mother kept talking about him so I knew he was working in England with a big company that was building motorways, power stations and hydro-dams. She would tell me: "If it wasn't for your father and the money he sends home, I don't know how we would get along."

I came to read the relief on her face when the postman delivered the letter with the stamp of the Queen's head in the top right hand corner and my father's tight writing below it. And I came to understand that I should leave her alone on the days when she stood like a sentry by the window looking out crestfallen each time the postman cycled past.

Our farm wasn't big, about 16 scattered acres in all, with a few fields close to the house and barns and the rest in the 'far land', a whin-studded outcrop half a mile away. It was just about enough to keep two milk cows, a few bullocks for selling and small fields to grow meadow for hay, oats and potatoes. I had my small jobs to do every day, sneaking into the hens' shed to collect eggs, shouldering bags of turf and logs for the fire and drawing buckets of water from the spring well.

So the build up to my father coming home was a welcome distraction. There was a bit of excitement and giddiness, mother telling me and my older brothers, Seán and Kevin, and sister Mary we needed to spruce the place up. Out we went slashing down briars and nettles around the haggard and skimming weeds from along the front walls of the house.

There was a fixed routine to his journey back home. We didn't have a car so once the date for his return was set, I was sent off up the village to book Joe Mac's small green Anglia van to take us on the six mile trip to Castlebar train station.

When the big day arrived my mother, Eileen, lined us up well before Joe Mac's van chugged up to the house and made sure, no matter how much squirming we did, that all our faces were scrubbed to angelic brightness with a towel lathered in Lifebuoy soap. She never came with us to the train station, always fussing about and saying she had too many things to get ready.

Joe was a small, stout jovial man who liked telling stories and then rippling with laughter at how funny his own yarns were. I liked him. He made me laugh. He was a part-time builder and so when he was on a job the passenger seat in the van was taken out to make more space to transport supplies.

There was always a right jostling match as we piled into the van as everyone wanted the front seat view. I got it that December day and ended up sitting on backside-numbing bags of cement. It was a small van so if you ended up in the back it was a case of crouching on your hunkers and pressing hands against the roof to keep balance as it swayed towards the town. Joe always drove, summer or winter, sun or blizzard, with the driver's window down and his right elbow stuck well out.

On the station platform I watched as the train rounded the bend, hissed and grinded to a halt. Steam of some sort spewed out low and people from the train emerged hazily through it. My father, the big brown suitcase in one hand and his overcoat slung across his other elbow, always recognised Joe Mac first and then turned towards us. His first stop when he arrived was Moran's pub. It was like a kind of ritual. Many of those gathered there were themselves just home from working in England. Men in wide pinstriped brown suits, hair Brylcreemed down, beads of sweat trickling and slowly darkening shirt collars. Some of them spoke a bit strange as faint hints of dialects from places like Lancashire and Yorkshire kept creeping in to distort the broad Mayo accent.

In the pub the fire crackled and spat out little eruptions of sparks as the turf sods collapsed into it. Grey cigarette smoke dwindled towards the yellowing ceiling.

I sipped my bottle of orange as the conversations swirled around me. I caught scraps of them as men boasted about or blackguarded Wimpey's, McAlpine's, Murphy's or Taylor Woodrow, the big firm my father worked for. There were fellas from my home village who talked as if they were engineers about hydro-dams, power stations, undergrounds, motorways as wide as ten Mayo roads put together, laying hot asphalt, hoppers and RB-10s, whatever they were. Big rolls of pound notes were dug out of trouser pockets. In one corner, below a painting of Robert Emmet making his speech from the dock, two florid-faced men wrestled over who would buy the next round of drinks.

Pints were guzzled and the talk was all the time about 'over there' and spiteful bosses, Irish gangers who turned on their own, landladies, good and awful digs, horses, pubs and the craic. Then a small, wiry man with a Woodbine dangling from his lower lip, suddenly stood up on a chair beside me and silenced the babble when he thrust his pint high in the air and, shouted: "Let's drink to the lost men of the West, the lads who didn't make it through this year over there." When he got down I could see tears edging down the furrows in his weather-beaten face.

Strange as it may seem, even as a six-year-old, I had an inkling as to why he was crying. I remembered months earlier sitting in a car with mother and the rest of the family somewhere on the Mayo border. It was dark and wet. The car wipers were lazily swiping away the rainy tears on the windscreen. I was confused when my father suddenly emerged out of the dense drizzle. It was not his time of year for coming home. He hugged my mother for a long time and said quietly to us children: "We'll all stand outside by the car. They'll be taking your Uncle Martin past in a few minutes.

We'll say a prayer together for him." A few minutes later a hearse drove slowly past taking Martin, my father's younger brother, home for the last time. Mother quietly explained to us that Martin had been deep down digging a trench on a building site in England when it began to cave in. He had a small hearing defect so when the shout went up for everyone to get out he heard it a fraction later than the other men and never escaped.

After leaving Moran's pub, we arrived home. My mother was standing in the doorway when Joe Mac's van chugged around the bend at the village church and up the hill to our house. "Welcome back, welcome home," she said, over and over, as my father and her hugged and kissed.

I turned away, embarrassed and a bit put out by all the fuss and attention he was getting. That was what made the first few days so awkward. The routine all of us had followed week in and week out was upset. There was now a man of the house, a man who was taking over the little jobs I did every day around the house and farm. He was carrying bigger rope-filled bundles of hay to the cattle in our far fields than I could manage. He pulled on wellingtons and cleared clogged ditches to free up drinking water for the animals, timber posts were driven deeper to make barbed wire fences sturdier and he had a great knack for fixing barn doors and getting lopsided gates to swing free again.

All the time I wanted to get closer to him but didn't know how. I watched our ageing sheepdog Bingo circle him, sniff and walk away without wagging his tail in greeting. My favourite cow, Daisy, was nervy and shifty to his touch when he began milking her.

One day, walking back from the spring well with my mother, we put our buckets down and stopped for a rest half-way up the narrow grass-crowned road. "You'll have to be nice to your father," she said quietly. "It's not easy on him. He's not here to see all the little things happening in your life. We'll all have to make him feel at home."

Sometimes I would stare from the hallway at him as he was shaving in the mirror above the kitchen sink, still in his white vest and with galluses hanging loose, and wish he would go away soon. Once he turned and saw me.

"When are you going back to England?" I had blurted out before feeling guilty for saying it. He took a towel and wiped off the residues of shaving soap, smiled a little and said: "Not long, another week. Don't worry, you'll have your mother all to yourself again soon. Maybe someday you'll have an idea of how hard all this is for me. Now run along and help your mother."

It was always in the second week of his stay that my childish huffs began to dilute and I started to enjoy being with him. He told me about cowboy films he had seen in England, the places he had worked and even asked me to help him predict the results of games for the English football pools competition he did every week.

And then, just as I felt we were melting slowly into a complete family, like the ones I saw at Mass on Sundays, it was time for him to go. I came to know the tell-tale signs. A full line of his shirts flapping and straining on the clothes line, the suitcase taken down from the top of the wardrobe, a last day out in Castlebar. At night lying in bed I could hear mother and father talking in low, serious tones below me in the kitchen, clutching at words of reassurance. "Sure the months will fly by. We'll write to each other."

As Joe Mac's van revved loudly outside he would hug each of us and make us promise to help our mother and to be good at school. "I'll see you all soon, please God," he would say, hurrying to leave and hide any tears. "Sure the months will fly by."

And then he was gone. We never went with him to the train. Joe Mac's van freewheeled down the hill, jerked as he forced it into gear and growled on. We all stood in the middle of the road and waved and kept on waving even after the bend at the church had swept my father, the van and, lastly, Joe Mac's elbow from view.

Tom Rowley is a native of Parke, near Castlebar, Co Mayo, and is a freelance writer and public relations consultant. A former senior journalist with 'The Irish Independent' and later a Government media advisor, he is married with two children and lives in Dublin.

AROUND THE FARM GATE

2 The Threshing

Dan Daly

IT was a truly wondrous sight for a four-year-old to behold. The huge lumbering salmon-coloured outline of the threshing machine made its way in the narrow little roadway to the farmyard. It rattled the branches of the ash trees as it rumbled over the gravel. A big faded-red tractor built like an elephant pulled it.

I can't recall a single one of those September days when the sun didn't shine on threshing day. The world always seemed warm and yellow. A 'meitheal' of neighbours – as many as 10 – had gathered in the yard, and were chatting and watching as Tangney's towering yellow thresher was manoeuvred into position alongside the ricks of barley that had mellowed and rested in the autumn sunshine for weeks.

The excitement had begun weeks earlier when the reaper 'n' binder – an exciting sight in itself – had come to cut the barley. I followed it as it slowly cut a swathe through the crackling barley and methodically and regularly kicked out the bound sheaves with a heavy click. My father and a few helpers followed, stooking quietly as they went. The dog ran around excitedly as I dashed from stook to stook. The stubble stung my feet.

Tangneys of Castlemaine threshed from September right through until St. Patrick's Day and sometimes beyond. They progressed westwards along the Castlemaine-Dingle road on the Dingle Penninsula through Boolteens, Keel, Inch and on as far as Dingle.

To my mind, it appeared to be a magical journey to wonderful places with a fascinating machine. They threshed some of the corn on the westward trip and the remainder on the homeward journey when the grain was well and truly ready. The great threshing odyssey was punctuated with sing-songs and harvest parties and none was as lively as when they reached Dingle.

The big belt was connected from the tractor to the thresher and it soon looped into action. A loud humming noise built up and filled the yard. Mick Enright and my father piked the sheaves from the rick onto the thresher. The twine was cut and the sheaf was fed into the drum. The grain sacks were filled and carried to the shed. The grain felt cool as it poured through my fingers into the sack. At the other end of the thresher, a couple of men heaped the straw onto a new rick.

The oats were always my favourite. Its straw, grain and chaff had a soft, smooth quality. The chaff from the barley used to stick to my clothes and tickle me. I was quickly covered with the stuff. I needed a rest and headed for the kitchen.

The table was laden with food of all sorts. There was white and brown bread, butter, thick slices of ham and brown sauce. Pots sizzled on the cooker. Mother and Mrs Carroll headed out with mugs of tea and slices of thick currant bread. Bottles of stout were produced. My father wiped the sweat from his forehead and downed one. Chaff and dust danced in the beams of mellow light that shone through the big ash tree in the corner. There was a golden warm atmosphere in the yard.

My father cracked a match and lit a cigarette. "Mind where you throw that match, Paddy," joked Mick Enright.

"We don't want a conflagration," added Pat Shea.

Suddenly my father started jumping up and down on the rick. At the same time Patrick Hickey fumbled in the barley for the fag that had fallen out of his grasp. He threw it into the ditch and stamped on the straw to stifle the flames. It had the makings of a wondrous duet as father then began to twitch and slap his trousers vigorously.

He had the stage and everyone's attention as he shook, twisted and danced in the manner of an intoxicated Indian high on firewater or a crazed Morris dancer. He shouted something along the lines of "the divil take ya" and fell on his back on the barley. He then sat up. Strands of barley were stuck to his hair. He looked like an agricultural Stan Laurel. The silent bemusement of the onlookers had given way to curious laughter.

"What's up, Paddy?"

"A bloody mouse ran up the leg of my trousers," he replied as he looked around.

"And where is he?"

"Devil if I know," he replied to a burst of laughter as he gave his trousers another slap.

"Here Paddy, put that on your head," said Jim Cronin, handing him a bottle of stout.

"I think you'll need something stronger than that," advised Mick Enright as he headed into the back kitchen. He returned with a bottle of whiskey and a few mugs. He poured Paddy a drink. He swilled it in the mug and savoured a deep draught. He wiped his brow and took another swallow.

"God Paddy, you'd go to any length for a proper drink," said Pats Shea.

"Well I don't want to go through that again, the little shagger."

"Kitty said you can never dance when she's around."

"Well here's to the harvest, Paddy and the mouse!"

They clicked mugs and laughed.

Soon they were back at work. My father now had his trouser legs tied with two pieces of blue binder twine. There was half a rick of barley still to thresh. And when the last sheaf had been tossed and the dust had settled they sat in the shade of the new rick of straw, pulled the heads off a few bottles, passed around the cigarettes and rested. There was a contented silence for a while.

"I wonder is he any relation?" inquired Mick Enright.

"Who?" asked my father.

"The mouse," he replied.

"What are you on about?"

"I wonder is that mouse any relation to the fellow who started the great Chicago fire?" inquired Mick.

"T'anam don diabhal, that wasn't a mouse. 'Twas a cow kicked over Mrs O'Leary's lamp," Dad informed him.

"I could have sworn it was a mouse. The memory plays strange tricks. Well it could have been just as serious. As Pats said we could have had a conflagration."

"The divil take him."

There was a contented chuckle.

The yard was suffused with a gentle, golden glow. The rick of straw had risen to touch the lowest branches and was having the finishing touches applied. The bags of barley were stacked high in the shed.

They chatted and joked for a while and then answered the call to head in for supper. Soon Tangneys and their enchanting machine departed, rattling the ash branches as they went. They left a void and a mound of chaff.

I felt a little sadness as the neighbours vanished into the

evening, their names echoing in farewell. There was a strange silence in the yard – not even a rustle. Beyond the yellow rick, through the great ash tree I could see the setting sun, large and golden, ripening Slieve Mish's heather to a flaxen bloom.

Dan Daly is a native of Kerry but lives in Robinstown, Navan, Co Meath. A recently retired primary school principal, he is married with three children. He writes as a hobby.

3 Horsemen Passing By

Edward Cunningham

THE horse's name was Benny. He was a big, easy-going grey. He was 12. I was three. My father was 53.

I was clinging to my father like a huggy bear and digging my little legs as tightly as I could into Benny's flanks.

It was my first time on his back. I was terrified, but at the same time proud and excited because, after all, that was my daddy riding that big horse and I was up behind him.

I had him all to myself. It was just us.

It was awful high up, though; I felt I had been borne to a strange, elevated realm. One where horse and man occupied a place and a life of their own. The world I'd lived in until then looked different from up there.

The strange thing is I've forgotten most of the details of my first journey on Benny. Yet I still, strangely, feel the sense of wonder.

There also was that sense of being close, so tight-close to the man with the battered, raggedy half-coat and the cocktail of scents and smells from that old garment: Of tobacco and cow dung and milk and grass and the half-wetness of drizzle from which he never sought shelter.

We were coming back up Bentley's narrow lane, which led to four-and-a-half bushy acres at the end of the pokey route alongside the Little River.

Daddy had to dodge the grappling, spitting-wet bushes,

briars and low-hanging branches, ducking here, swaying there. I'd laugh when he'd get splattered as my tiny piggybacking body clung like a limpet to his muscular frame and shadowed his every horse-stride movement.

I don't remember much more about that day – even now it is a sense – and probably wouldn't even be able to recall the little I can were it not for him becoming so animated over something that I knew nothing about.

He, a quiet man who never exaggerated or gilded the lily, was to take great pride in telling of a strange moment.

To me what he said had happened was a thing of nothing at the time. But my father saw it differently and over the years his words inexorably imprinted importance on it for me.

And now, at this remove, it lingers like few other moments from my young life. It is, betimes, tantalisingly close to being tangible.

When you are young you are oblivious to the small things. When you are older, they dredge much more than nuggets of nostalgia.

They re-attach and re-align you to a time, a place, a culture, a way of life and, most importantly for me, a man, a hero, a dreamer, a gentleman and a miner of nature at it richest seam.

The great irony is that even though I was half petrified on Benny's back, I never felt more secure than that day. And possibly haven't since.

I knew my daddy would make sure nothing happened.

Only it did, you see.

And that little happening was to span a lifetime in the simple significance my father bestowed on it.

After counting the few sheep and cattle in the front field we were making an uneventful return back up to civilisation.

We chatted all the way up along the lane and as we neared the rickety gate that opened from Bentley's mucky passageway onto the Moate Road, Benny slipped a little on the rutted, slimy surface. For a split second, he sought a more secure footing.

In doing so we were jolted just a little – like you would be if someone unexpectedly tapped the brakes of a car while cruising along.

It was only a second but, apparently, in that moment and movement my chin cracked into my father's lower back.

He was a sturdy, physically rock-hard man but the contact melted him. Not physically; he didn't know the meaning of fear or real pain.

However, in the nudge of his eldest son's chin, there was for him a profoundly deeper significance.

We were back on the tarred road in seconds, his great strong left-arm arching back to circle my little body with a fiercely protective grip despite Benny's re-asserted steadiness.

I have a recollection of Daddy looking closely at me as he hoisted me down from Benny's back before hugging me.

He was a deeply loving man but parents didn't hug children much in those days or tell them they loved them. I remember him becoming animated.

He held Benny's mane with his left hand and hugged me again with his right. "Nedser," he said and dropped his gaze to the ground. (He used to call me Ned of the Hills).

"Nedser," he repeated looking back up at me with half-shut eyes. "When I was your age, I rode back up that lane at my daddy's back on a big, white horse."

Even as a three-and-a-bit-year-old I sensed emotion in a grown up. I'd never seen that sort before.

He was talking to me like I was big enough, old enough to understand. I was frightened, embarrassed a little but almighty conscious that I, unknowingly, had somehow been the harbinger of something truly important for him.

And when you love someone and have that effect as a child, it brings a strange, inexplicable, feeling to play.

I can remember how he lifted his face back up, how he shook his head in disbelief and how he pushed his cap back further on his head.

"And the white horse slipped exactly where Benny did just now," he continued, "and I cracked my chin into my father's back in exactly the same place you did."

He laughed; a wistful, warm laugh. "And that was 50 years ago. I remember my daddy telling me, like I'm telling you now."

When we got home he told my mother, and for the following days, weeks, months and years, anyone who would listen. People had time to talk those days and nights. And even when they didn't he'd bring it up now and again, especially around my birthday.

What I loved about him, though, was he never embellished what happened – at least as far as I could tell.

People would nod their heads and look at me.

At first I felt a bit weird, but as the years brought a little more reflective maturity I've come to realise how a simple, second-long slip from a horse and a little nudge of my chin forged an eternal bond across three generations of my family.

Edward Cunningham grew up on a small farm in Clara, Co Offaly. A father of four, he is an author and former deputy editor of the 'Irish Independent' newspaper

4 A Turf Saving Deliverance

Noreen Brennan-Donoghue

I HAD not seen him in years, yet strangely I knew him at once. It seemed as if I was transported back in time, to another life, another world.

It was all so familiar, the sun was hot and reflecting back off the heather, a haze seemed to linger in the air. The bird song was clear as crystal, the warm wind, whirling up tiny dust storms. A short distance away smoke curled sideways in the breeze, stinging my eyes, and a feeling of hunger came over me. The shouts of my brothers and sisters seemed muted and far away.

My mother came round the corner on her new Raleigh bicycle, the handlebars laden with shopping bags. However, it was not shopping that the bags held, but a feast for the hungry workers. Fresh sodabread, covered with butter, chunks of cheese and bottles of tea kept warm in woollen socks.

I was on top of the bank nearest the road, and he was beneath me on the cutaway. He was crouched down facing me and was wearing his green jumper, his dark trousers and his black wellingtons. My gaze was drawn to his long hands, as they were the first time I saw him.

It was a cold March day and my sister and I had cycled to Ballymote to see our new born brother. There was a coating of frost on the blue gloves I had worn, I had knitted them myself and they were ill-fitting and tight. I remember stretching out my hand to stroke his tiny ear, and I marvelled at how long his fingers were. It was love at first sight, a love that would last forever.

He looked towards me then and smiled, a smile I thought I would never see again, and my heart was glad to see him and my spirits soared skywards with the lark. I jumped down onto the cutaway and went forward to enclose him in my embrace. He held me close and I rested my face on his chest. I could hear his heart beating, his breath warm on my head. He was tall, with the build of our father. I told him it was so good to see him, to hold him once more. Dad shouted to us to stop our chattering and come and have our tea.

Our turf bank was two miles away from our home in Doocastle; it came with the chimney of the old house purchased by my grandfather in 1929. Saving the turf was a hard job that took months from the clearing of the bank in March to bringing it home in the autumn.

In preparation for the turf cutting my father would load the ass and cart with all the tools for the job. Spade, shovel, slean and wheelbarrow.

The slean was a tool specially designed to slice through the wet turf and gave hand cut turf its distinctive shape. The slean could be designed for a right handed person or a "ciotóg", a left handed person.

The squelch of turf torn from the earth by the slean, from where it has rested in tranquillity for centuries, flew upwards from the sunken bank, and was briefly caught by my brother and guided onto the waiting wheelbarrow. John wheeled the turf out onto the bank; it was later scatted, turned and then footed.

The turf was "put out" from the bank and left at a convenient siding near the road from where it was taken home by donkey and cart. The smaller children travelled to the bog in the ass's cart with father, its iron wheels grinding the small stones and lumbering into potholes making the ride experience.

The two oldest ones were lucky enough to cycle. A donkey and cart was borrowed from a neighbour so that there was always a full cart ready for the people who were driving the donkeys. A neighbour might come and give a helping hand, a favour returned by my father or my brother or we might "owe" a neighbour a day and help them with some other work at a later date.

One soon learned that it was best to stay up wind of the fillers, as a piece of turf mould in the eye was a lesson one did not forget in a hurry. The bog hole was another trap for the unwary, lurking with its still dark water with only the odd dragon fly to disturb its calm, but underneath we were warned, was a glue like substance that once you stepped into its clutches only the lucky would escape from. Depending on the amount of turf, the help available and the weather this task might take one or two days to complete. Once the turf was out Dad would bring it home at his leisure, taking one or two ass-carts into the school for winter fuel, as was the custom at the time.

The others did not join us for our feast, and so, Mum, Dad, myself and Gabriel sat down up wind of the turf fire that Dad had built. We did not do much more work that day; we sat and talked of days long past, of people who had gone on into God's keeping and the neighbours in our daily life.

I sat close to Gabriel holding his hand and the sadness of his absence for so many years seemed to melt away like snow in warm sunlight. My mother seemed younger, and carefree. My father shed the burden of sorrow that had bent his shoulders, and was truly the father of my youth.

We talked on and soon the sun lost its warmth as it made its slow decent to sleep in the West. We tidied away the remains of our feast, we dampened down our glowing fire with wet scraws and prepared to cycle home. Our conversation continued, stirring within me, peace, contentment and happiness. As we cycled around the last turn, our house stood solid against the darkening sky, the cows lowing in the well field as they awaited milking. The hens, ducks, turkeys and geese complained loudly about their lack of supper. My father, mother and brother walked in through the back door and out of my line of sight.

I awoke with a start to a cold winter's morning, my heart hammering loudly in my chest, and tears of loss on my cheeks. My dream was peopled with the ghosts of my loved ones long dead, the images of my former life bringing me solace for a few moments until reality returned.

I had once more to mourn the loss of my much loved brother, who died when we were children.

Noreen Brennan-Donoghue is a native of County Sligo. Married with four sons, she is a barrister who likes to write as a hobby.

5 The Great Turnip Swindle of 1955

Robert Leonard

IT was 1955 in the middle of Meath when the summer days appeared long to teenagers facing hard days thinning turnips.

At half seven in the morning, I cycled a few miles with three friends up a long avenue smothered in trees where we fell in with about a dozen other young boys.

A big farmhouse stood proudly at the top of the laneway but the narrow road branched off before we got to it and led up to a farmyard. The house and all the surrounding fields were owned by a rich farmer who hired the youngsters of the locality for this seasonal work.

We congregated in the farmyard on this first day of work. There were four large brown workhorses poking their heads over the half-doors of the stone stables. At the end of the stables was living accommodation for the farmhand, though it was built of the same stone as the sheds and had the same slate roof.

Even in high summer, there was a smell of turf smoke as the farm worker boiled the kettle for his morning tea over an open fire. He came out and directed us towards a long field to commence the work.

He left us to the thinning while he went off with more experienced workers to cut and turn hay in other fields.

We knew this field well from toiling in it the previous autumn picking potatoes. Now it was yielding a different vegetable but the job would be just as horrible.

Thinning turnips involved crawling on your knees between the drills, pulling all the weeds and young turnip plants out to leave just one turnip plant standing approximately every twelve inches. This would allow these plants to grow to maturity without competition.

We were each allocated a number of long drills. The work was hard and dirty and we would normally get through two drills a day and end it with aching limbs and skin peeled from our fingers. It would take a week to complete the field and we got paid two shillings per drill when the work was over.

Payday was on Sunday. It was suspicious that this Protestant farmer chose to pay his casual workers at the same time Mass was on in the Catholic Church.

Anyhow, the money/Mass argument was easily won, even with the most pious mothers and we would sit waiting outside the big house for a couple of hours until he delivered our wages.

All of us came from the parish and we worked honestly and efficiently but there was one exception this year, a boy who bore a grudge.

Let's call my friend Jumbo after the famous circus elephant, because elephants never forget. Jumbo had picked potatoes with us the previous year but just two days of worn hands and filthy fingernails made him decide that this wasn't the job for him.

On the Sunday that we were to be paid he came along with the rest of us and lined up to get his dues for the two days he had worked. Jumbo's face went red with anger when he was told that he wouldn't be getting any money as he had failed to complete the job like the rest had done.

Surprisingly, this June the one boy who seemed to take to thinning turnips like he was born to do it was Jumbo.

He was up and down those drills like a hare, hands working in a blur of action. He was miles ahead of the rest of us and despite our best efforts, we just couldn't keep up with him.

On those hot, muggy days we were eaten by midges and bothered by flies, particularly when working on a drill close to the heavy hedges.

The insects flew down from the hawthorn and elder bushes to make a feast of our poor sweaty skin.

Around lunchtime we stopped to unwrap slices of a white loaf spread with butter and jam and washed it down with milk, raw from the cow, that we brought in a glass bottle with a cork wedged in it. It tasted warm but delicious and much creamier than pasteurised milk.

One of the boys asked Jumbo to share his technique but he just smiled. I studied him through the day and finally worked out what he was doing. He was ripping everything up from the ground in one foul swoop instead of weeding and picking around a single plant. Then he burrowed a little hole in the ground and stuck one of the uprooted turnips back in to make it appear that it was growing normally.

There was no way of immediately spotting what he had done but in the not too distant future the evidence would be plain to see.

At around six in the evening we finished up for the day and headed back home, tired and hungry but happy in that we were making a good wage for the week.

That Sunday we cycled up the laneway, chatting excitedly. The usual long wait took some of the energy out of us but finally the farmer came out and proceeded to dole out the spoils. Jumbo's whole body seemed to smile as he stuck out his hand to accept his wages.

That wasn't the last time I visited that field that year. I couldn't resist nipping down for a look when the turnips began to grow. What stood out like a sore thumb was Jumbo's empty drills of rootless turnips that had perished – leaving bare swathes through the heavy-leafed crop.

He had taken his revenge!

Robert Leonard is a native of Wilkinstown, Co. Meath. He is married with four children and seven grandchildren.

6 A Spot Of Dust

Joe Kearney

WITH time everything returns to dust.

Not long ago, I watched on TV from the comfort of my living room, as a satellite came safely to rest on the dry floor of the Utah desert. The cargo it contained was truly wondrous, a handful of stardust from the outer edges of our universe; a fistful of the very stuff we are made from.

Dust to dust.

But the good news was a mere sound bite; it was followed by the usual litany of sorrows and disaster. I was however, intrigued by the small satellite that contained the debris. Following its long seven year journey and fiery re-entry into the earth's atmosphere, it resembled some long defunct piece of farm machinery.

A vessel that might have been part of a milking machine from the sixties for example; something that would have been overtaken by polished stainless steel and finally dumped between the rusted shafts of an old hay-rake where docks and nettles might soften its battered shape and cushion its rest. As sometimes happens, the images from deep space awakened memories.

The year 1957 had a wet summer. In the fields, swathes of hay had been so frequently turned they resembled mildewed drifts of mouldering seaweed blown inland on the breath of an angry storm. The corn was slow to ripen and turf-cutting virtually abandoned. Something had to be wrong in the world. The weather gods were offended. Raise your eyes from the fields of our small community and what was visible was not Mount Olympus but Slievenaman; throughout that summer sporting a persistent cap of dampened cloud. The elders and wise men of the locality waited patiently for St Swithin's day.

They would gauge the remainder of the season by events on that particular feast-day. Popular belief was that if it rained on that day then it would do so for a biblical span of forty days and forty nights. The feast-day came and sun shone down on the dampened fields like a golden benediction. A brisk breeze swept in from the west and ruffled the upper strands of hay, the ears of corn and the sodden contents of washing lines. Hearts soared; gods, saints and nature were once again appeased. But on the following day and the following day and the one after that again, the heavens opened, rain returned and the cap was once more resettled upon the head of Slievenaman.

It was much later in the year before we came to understand what had happened. The same elders and wise men reported seeing a new star in the sky. Newspapers reported that the Russians had instigated an artificial satellite programme. And we had a new word to play with. It had all the sibilance and glottal resonance of a swearword, yet you could spit it out in public and not receive a clip across the ear... Sputnik!

All this was happening at a time when my grandmother included a trimming in the nightly rosary for the conversion of Russia.

When we knelt in the kitchen with the fire scorching our backs, as if reminding us of the very flames of hell, there hanging on a hook, inside the door was the government information booklet advising us of what precautions we should take to survive nuclear fall-out in the event of receiving a direct hit from an atomic bomb.

To relieve the boredom of prayer I imagined what it might be like to spend two weeks underneath the kitchen table with just Granny for company. I sincerely prayed that the bomb might never fall.

On November 3, 1957, Sputnik 2 was launched. It carried the first living passenger into space, a dog named Laika. But the mission planners had not provided for either the safe return of dog or spacecraft and Laika became the first space casualty. Later on in the programme two more dogs, Belka and Strelka, along with 40 mice and two rats were launched on board Sputnik 5. On this occasion, you will be relieved to learn, both craft and animals were recovered safely following their brief space journey.

But back in 1957, when the elders and wise men discovered that there was a dog in space, they finally understood the cause of the wet summer. Above the mutterings of the rosary I often heard Mikey Maher's greyhounds lift their muzzles to the sky and now understand that they were sending up long howling lamentations of sympathy for the dog lost in space. We discovered afterwards that all Sputniks were carried into orbit by the R-7 launch rocket, originally designed to carry nuclear warheads.

Time, global enlightenment and perhaps even Granny's prayers rendered the fall-out survival booklet redundant. We never needed to test our tolerance of each other in enforced incarceration beneath the kitchen table.

I recalled our days of marvel at early space exploration when I saw that spacecraft land in the Utah desert. It also brought me back to a lost time in London in the late 1960s.

On July 20, 1969, in the Crown public-house in Cricklewood, I watched through a haze of roll-up-smoke the crew of Apollo 11 walk on the moon. As spectators, in the Crown, we shared much in common with astronauts Neil Armstrong and "Buzz" Aldrin, we too were kitted out in a form of 'moon-boots.'

The exception was, however, ours kept us more firmly secured to the surface of England than we would have wished. Our construction hobnails were burdened with the muck of the London trenches and that, conjoined with lumpen gravity, ensured that we remained earthbound and did not seek to soar beyond our situation.

On that day in the Crown, I had worry-beads of a sort in my shirt pocket. I was at that time a drifter, a piece of dust at the whim of fate, capable of being easily blown off course. A couple of days previously, a blue envelope had found me. It contained three lined sheets of Basildon Bond notepaper. The handwriting was unmistakable; my mother's.

The heavy-handed script taught to her by the Mercy nuns had been pressed into the paper by her blue pen so hard it seemed as brail when I fingered the letter in my pocket. It was written with love but you had to find the sentiment between the lines; that's the sort of family we were.

"It was a good year for the early spuds but Tobin's bull had broken into the garden and trampled the carrot and cabbage bed. Young Alice, down the road, had gone to Australia to take up nursing. The family were worried about when they might see her again."

We never voiced our own wishes and desires but instead chose to express them, obliquely, through the lives of others.

The envelope was one of a packet of 24 that she would have bought at Kerwicks newsagents. I calculated that by the time they were used up we would be into a new year and Christmas would have passed.

Would I be home? In my pocket rattled just one entrance fee to the Sea of Tranquillity and unless the winds of fortune blew more favourably, home would be as far removed as Australia or the moon.

I took the letter out again. On the TV screen we were long past the moment where Armstrong had told us all about 'small steps' and 'giant leaps'.

As I refolded the notepaper, I noticed stuck to the back of the third sheet was a solitary breadcrumb. When my mother had written, the passion of her enterprise against the unyielding surface of the worn oilcloth had forced an overlooked crumb to adhere to the letter.

I picked it off, this small particle of home and tasted it. It was hard and stale but it was the closest I had been to the kitchen table in a long time and I stared wide-eyed at the grey flickering images until I was certain that I could command the tears to remain unshed.

There were men on the moon. We were stardust and I was but one slight speck in the whole universe.

However, I know now, what I did not know then... that dust, even the dust of ancient, deepest space, eventually settles.

Dr Joe Kearney is a native of Callan, Co Kilkenny. He worked for most of his life in the oil industry but is now concentrating on writing and has produced his first novel 'Moon Blind.'

AROUND THE FARM GATE

7 The Murhur Reel

John Dillon

LIFE on the land was always hard whether you were working for a farmer or were a farmer yourself. My uncle was a farmer. He was neither a big farmer nor a small farmer. He had about 15 cows but to tell the truth he didn't worry too much about farming if there was a session playing the fiddle on offer.

If there was a mention of a shindig Paddy Maloney, my uncle, and the Maneen Cronin would be playing at it. They were both fiddle players. Sometimes Sonny McCarthy would join in with the melodeon.

They were an oddly assorted team. Paddy was short and very thin. He'd have no problem going through the eye of the needle and getting into heaven even if he were a rich man, which he was not.

Sonny McCarthy was small and squat and the Maneen was at least 6' 4" without an ounce of fat. Their usual arrangement was that the Maneen sat in front of a table and the other two sat on the table behind him. Paddy and Sonny always had a glass of porter alongside them or a mug. The Maneen, strangely enough, did not drink.

Wherever they went to play Paddy did a solo turn called the Murhur Reel. It was his reel and the Maneen never played it or anyone else for that matter. It was a haunting tune. No matter what kind of a crowd was there and no matter what drink was taken, they would fall silent.

Paddy was a good but not exceptional fiddle player; the Maneen was considered better. But when playing the Murhur Reel, Paddy seemed inspired. Why he called it a reel I don't know because I never saw anyone dance when he played it.

It started off slowly and sweetly, then it had a faintly crying sound before changing back to a happy quick tempo. Then it finished on a solemn and serious note again.

Almost profound, it was hard to describe... mellow perhaps. Sonny McCarthy described it as a twelve-year-old whiskey at that point. Near the end the fiddle went wild or Paddy went wild. It was like a storm blowing. Sweat poured out of my uncle. Christy Moore had nothing on him. And then it died away like a summer breeze. Gentle notes. And always Paddy would say: "I play this for Ger Kelleher, God rest his soul."

Sometime people would ask Paddy where he got the tune and he would reply: "It's a long story and I'll tell you some other time." And some people would ask why he called it: "The Murhur Reel". But they never got an answer.

My uncle was a master of evasion. He had an old sheep dog called Sailor. My mother used to say that he told Sailor everything because he knew the dog wouldn't talk. And my father would say: "That bloody dog is getting so crafty it wouldn't't surprise me if he did."

As it transpired, I managed to find out where he got the tune though the pity is that it is now lost forever.

Paddy loved Sailor. They were great company for each other on the land. His wife, Nancy, never went out of doors. She was a great cook always making the most of everything. But she never went out, not even on a Sunday.

She complained of a bad chest though she lived to a great age. Though never out, she knew everybody's business sometimes better than themselves. I think now she had a great memory and a lot of people were in and out of the house as my uncle liked company.

Nancy asked them plenty of questions and she gave them tea and cake and asked them more questions. She could entertain the queen.

Then she got a cat. The cat and dog sometimes got on together and sometimes did not. They were like humans. They were all about each other and suddenly, for no apparent reason, they were at it, well, like cats and dogs.

I was up at Paddy's house one evening at the end of May and just as I was going over the fields to bring the cows for milking I called Sailor to go with me. We were going out the back haggard when for no reason the dog went for the cat. The cat ran up the haggard and jumped up on the windlass of the well. Sailor, giving full chase, couldn't put on the brakes in time and went headlong down into the well.

I raised the alarm. Paddy came out of the stall where he had been nailing up part of a manger. When he realised what happened he was in a panic.

"We must get him out," he pleaded to me.

The cat had hightailed it from the scene. Paddy let down the bucket. Even now I can hear the rattle of the chain as Paddy unwound it furiously. He expected that Sailor would get into the bucket. "Get in boy, get in boy", he kept saying.

But the shock of the cold water must have fuddled the dog's brain. The hottest day of the year the water was as cold as ice. When that failed Paddy wound the bucket back up.

"Get in," he ordered me. "Hold on to the chain. Bring him up!"

I was only nine at the time but I had enough sense to say: "Are you mad?"

"I'll give you anything if you do it," he pleaded.

I knew Paddy thought a penny he'd give you was worth a £100.

"I'll do it if you tell me where you got the Murhur reel," I said.

"I will, I promise!" he said," I will tell you later."

"I heard you say that before to other people. You tell me now," I said, standing firm.

There and then he told me but only on a sworn promise that I never tell anybody until he was dead 20 years. He is dead 30 years now, having lived to be 95.

This was his story but in my translation: I couldn't tell it in Paddy's own words because he was so anxious to finish it and get me down for the dog that it was more than a bit garbled.

"If you ever travel the road between Listowel and Tarbert you can take a diversion to Moyvane. Along that road you'll see a sign for Murhur Graveyard. It so happened that many years ago Ger Kelleher was coming from Moyvane to Listowel.

"It was about 11 at night in the month of July. He had more than a few drinks on him and he felt he had to get to sleep. He turned the pony down the road towards the graveyard. The road is no more than a quarter of a mile long and when he got to the gate he hitched the pony to it and stretched out in the car and fell asleep. It wouldn't be his first time sleeping off too much drink by all accounts. Anyway he woke after an hour to the sound of a fiddle playing. It was coming from the graveyard. He was too frightened to stir until the music stopped.

"Three nights later he was at my uncle Paddy's and he told him the story and what was more, played the tune for him on the mouth organ. It seems he was an accomplished player of that instrument. Strangely enough, having played it once he forgot it. Like you might forget a dream, I suppose.

"The last time that tune was played was in 1947. January of that year was hard and cold and there was a lot of frost. My Uncle Paddy was out in the stall with a cow calving. On his way back in later on he slipped on the ice and he put out his hands to break the fall and the fingers of the left were damaged. Not badly but bad enough that he never played the fiddle again.

The Murhur Reel was lost back then as sure as Kerry lost the All-Ireland final to Cavan in the Polo Grounds in New York that autumn.

Of the two, in my opinion, the Murhur Reel was the greater loss.

John Dillon was born in 1930 and raised on a farm in Duagh, Co Kerry. A retired pharmacist, he is married with two grown-up children and two granddaughters.

8 A Love Story Of The Mountains

Tony McCormack

ANUMBER of years ago, I worked as a sales representative for a veterinary company. My brief was mainly in the midland counties but during winter time it also involved calling to farmers in North Western Ireland selling minerals blocks. Those I called to there were mainly sheep farmers who farmed the mountain commonages.

They were excellent farmers who had descended from generations of such people.

On my first visit, I aimed my car northwards up the mountains. Little did I know that over the following couple of months that I would play a small but significant part in reuniting two former lovers that were split for over 40 years.

It was on my first visit that I encountered John Wilson. His personal profile as provided to me from my predecessor was very positive. The entrance to the house was approached by a long laneway with gorse bushes rubbing the side of the car at every turn. Half-way up the 300 yard laneway, I was greeted by collie dogs, biting, barking and escorting me for the last stint of my journey.

John was about 70 years old, tall, fit looking and clean shaven. He was slow to call back the dogs until he recognised the Cork number plate. I slowly slinked out of the car as the collies retreated to the outhouse. He enquired about my predecessor, his current whereabouts and gave him in general a very good reference.

I went through the usual routine of discussing the weather, lamb prices and GAA. I knew not to go near politics. After about a half an hour of general chat, he asked me to call on him in about two weeks at which time he would be able to gauge his seasonal requirements.

The views of the mountains were spectacular. John's house was half way and the grey-stone across the valley was interspersed with gorse and green grass even at that time of year.

On my second arrival at John's house, the dogs retreated immediately, leading me to conclude that the first time he must have sent the dogs out to greet me just in case I was up to no good. The difference in the greeting was amazing.

"Good day Tony, I'd say you are freezing since leaving the lovely flat lands of County Meath. Come on in to my humble abode and don't mind the dogs," he said warmly.

John's hospitality would have come closer to the ratings of the married men as opposed to some of the dire ratings I have had to allocate to some of the single farmers.

He told me that he had lived all his life on the farm that had been passed on for generations. Unfortunately he was an only child who had never married so the line would end with him.

After an hour's conversation, I pulled out my laptop and proceeded to type in the order.

"Do you have the interweb on that thing," he enquired. I explained that the signal was not great but that it would work.

All of a sudden he took an interest in 'googling' so I explained how it worked and what it could do. His reaction was one of astonishment and wonder. He hastily stood up and to my amazement reduced his order of mineral blocks and asked me to come back again.

Two weeks later he was standing at the house and I knew by the expressions on his face that his mood was more sombre than when I had previously met him.

"Come on in Tony, I need to talk to you about something," he confided.

He began by ordering the balance of what he had cancelled as if to prove that he was not wasting my time.

When we concluded that, he sat down opposite me and began to recall his own love story that had gone astray. As a 20-year-old he had fallen for a local girl called Mary Casey. They had dated for a number of years and they were in love with each other, or so he thought, with plans to get married and move onto John's family farm.

John's mother disapproved of Mary for no good reason other than John was her only child. He and Mary decided to emigrate to America where they would make a new life safe from any interfering or unwanted attention.

Mary headed out first and the intention was that John would follow six months later when she had found a home and got settled. For days and weeks and months, he waited impatiently for a letter to arrive from the states with news of Mary's progress.

None came.

Finally, after six months he visited Mary's brother where he received the devastating news that she had not mentioned anything in her letters home about her plans to reunite with him.

John decided that Mary had wanted a clean break not just from the area, but also from John, and most definitely his mother.

The news affected his health and he turned to the bottle for a brief period before settling down to the lifestyle that he was still living to that day, some 40 years later.

"I've spent my whole life wondering how Mary got on. I'm wondering if you would you be able to check on the interweb to see if there are any details of her life since I last saw her," he asked sheepishly.

I hesitated. Seeing my reluctance, John assured me that he would be able to deal with whatever the search turned up.

On typing in Mary Casey, New York, I got about 2,000 hits so he provided me with her date of birth, which was still etched into his brain. This further refined my search and out popped an article on local artists. I read to him a summary detailing that Mary was on tour with her art exhibition. The reason that it was detailed was because the exhibition would have an Irish leg of the tour including a stop in Sligo.

John stood up, took a deep breath and walked around the kitchen.

"When is she in Sligo, Tony?"

"February 18th and 19th in the Exhibition Centre."

"That's my Mary alright, she was always painting even back then," he recalled. "I will go to see her, there are many questions that I need answered."

I knew that he needed some time to himself so I made my excuses and left him to plan his next move.

I called to John twice more the same winter and his mood had improved considerably though oddly, he never mentioned Mary to me again.

****

The following January I looked forward to meeting John to discuss the previous year's GAA championship and to see if there might be further word on Mary.

Driving up his laneway, I was surprised that I did not get my canine escort. When I got to the front of the house, it was apparent that it was derelict and had been that way for some time.

I drove down to John's neighbour, Owen, who asked me: "Were you the sales rep, that re-introduced John to Mary?"

"I am," I replied.

"Well, fair play to you, you helped that man die happy if there's such a thing," he said.

Owen filled in the blanks on what had happened. John organised Owen to give him a lift to Sligo to attend Mary's exhibition. He recognised her immediately and tentatively edged slowly towards her. On seeing John, Mary embraced him and after talking for a while, she promised to visit him at a more suitable location.

Over the following number of days Owen said he saw a taxi negotiate John's laneway staying for about an hour at a time. During these meetings, Mary told John of her life in America.

She was keen to explain her disappearance because she said it had weighed heavily on her mind. She said that it was the wrath of John's mother that had stopped her from writing to him as they had promised.

It transpired that the mother had found out about the elopement and had made a point of warning Mary not to take her son.

What pleased John most, according to Owen, was when she told him she hadn't married because she never found anyone as good as him.

John was never as content as in the last three months of his life – seemingly not even as much as when Leitrim won the Connacht football final in 1994, according to Owen.

He was found dead sitting on his chair beside the window overlooking the valley.

At his funeral the undertaker placed one large bouquet of flowers on the coffin. There was no name accompanying the message. This time there was no need.

Tony McCormack hails from Delvin, Co. Westmeath. Married with two children, he is a development officer with Westmeath Community Development, a part-time farmer and likes to write as a hobby.

9 Fair Day In Kildysart

Gearóid Ó Ciaráin

THE monthly fair of Kildysart punctuated life in that rural West Clare parish through the 1950s just as the telegraph poles punctuated our daily walk to and from school.

It was a particular godsend for us children as the school always closed for the fair day. I'm not quite sure if this practice arose from a concern for the children, many of whom would otherwise have to make their way through the cattle filled village or from a simple acceptance that the country boys were unlikely to turn up one way or the other.

From about half five in the morning you could see the faint light in the distance from the lanterns of Labasheeda farmers as they walked their cattle the seven or eight miles to Kildysart.

"Hhup! Kumon! Shtop her… " broke through the dawn as a young heifer tried to avail of any possible opportunity to bolt for home. Both man and beast settled into a certain level of tranquillity as they neared the village. There were fewer gaps in the ditches and the three laneways ahead all had shut gates.

The stout jobbers clad in their tan knee-length light coats held the fortune of the day in their hands. They bore a well-crafted stick with a ferrule, which could act as a walking stick, a pointer, or a cattle prod. These early risers tried to steal a march on their fellow jobbers by going out the road so as to get a first chance at the incoming cattle. These fellows would cod you up to the balls of your eyes if you weren't careful. They never used the simple 'God bless him' when referring to an animal but rather tried to make little of the beast and of his owner.

Two of these jobbers had the particularly obnoxious habit of waving wads of money in the faces of poor farmers to tempt them to part with their hard turned out animals for less than their full value.

"Are you selling?"

"Begor, I would if I got the right price."

"They're small with you."

"Ah, they're alright."

"What are you looking for for the little whitehead?"

"That's the makings of a fine bullock. I'd want to get 25 for him."

"You'll be waitin for it," the jobber would say, turning on his heel and walk on with a well-practised air of indignity.

"Well then, I'll bring him home without it."

And so on, to the cross and up to the village.

Each man herded his own cattle into little groups as best he could, keeping them apart from other cattle. Most of them had horns and the younger bullocks tended to get a little territorial. A good lash of an ash-plant across the head was required to break up duelling animals.

Fresh grass and milk in the bellies of young cattle produced some chemical reaction which emitted a gas causing the beast to swell. The cure was to stab them into the stomach with a sharp knife to release the gas.

The other side-effect of dewy fresh grass was to cause an animal to shoot a scour half the width of the street and it was such a volley that caused my father's only ever appearance before the local district court and his only time to feature in *The Clare Champion.*

There was always a tension between some non-shopkeeping residents of the village and the farmers that came to boiling point when a newly painted door got showered from beneath a heifer's tail and caused the resident to make a formal complaint to the local Garda sergeant.

On inspection an ancient bye-law was produced which forbade cattle from going onto the footpath. The sergeant had no option but to come and take the names of the law-breakers, my father among them. They were duly summoned to the next district court sitting which coincided with a fair day. Some of those summoned proposed pooling money to hire a solicitor to represent them.

My father objected, saying he would do it for them all. He happened to know the District Justice from meeting him in Pat Joe O'Dea's hostelry at lunchtimes at fairs.

It was with considerable confidence that my father spoke up on behalf of himself and his beleaguered friends. He said it would be impossible to keep cattle off the footpath and that any attempt to enforce such a law would amount to blackguarding farmers trying to sell their cattle at the fair.

He went on to claim that neither God nor man knew any way of stopping cattle from dunging wherever and whenever they felt like it. The Probation Act was applied and the matter was not revisited for as long as fairs lasted in the village.

I have digressed but will now return to the fair at early morning time.

The jobbers move freely until they see something that they fancy. They ask the price and make an offer which is far short of the asking price. Both men engage in psychological combat until each is sure that he has brought the other to near breaking point when the jobber could walk away. Then, in steps a tangler who will try to negotiate a compromise.

"What's between ye?"

"Ye'll split it."

"I won't."

"Go on, you will."

The jobber produces a raddle ready to put his mark on the beast if he gets the say so. And so the deal is about to be closed when the jobber demands a pound back for luck.

"Ten shillings is all 't'will be. You are getting him chape enough"

"Go on, fifteen shillings."

And the farmer reluctantly accepts the deal by his silence. The beast is raddled and if the jobber is a big enough dealer then he writes a ticket with the agreed price to be cashed later when the cattle are being loaded on to his lorry.

A small time dealer will face the wall and adopt the stance of a man about to relieve himself. Instead he pulls a wad of money from his back pocket and counts out the exact amount required leaving his onlookers with no idea of his total spending power for the day.

The Maloneys opened their house in the middle of the village for hungry men who had a need for sustenance by mid-morning. It only opened on fair days and for two shillings served a hearty breakfast of nouveau cuisine – slices of ham, tomatoes, white baker's bread and island butter.

There was no variation to the menu. Men sat next to each other on stools at a long table and discussed prices and current demand as they ate their share and washed it down with a good mug of tea and a woodbine.

Hawkers set up shop in the square using a light metal

frame at the back of their vans covered by green canvas and having wooden trays containing their wares tilted at a slight angle towards the customers.

They sold boots and wellingtons, spanners and clocks and new-fangled gadgets of dubious merit. Each item was in turn auctioned to the attendant audience.

Pubs could, by now, open their doors in the full sight of the law and those who were already well ensconced stood with an elbow on the counter guarding their glasses of stout and small whiskeys. The peaked caps still covered their foreheads and the buttons on the overcoats were closed up.

This could take a while, but no matter. In such a convivial environment could stories be told, of a banbh bought or a match suggested for an eligible man of whatever means.

Just another pole on the road to eternity...

Gearóid Ó Ciaráin was born and reared on a small farm in the West Clare parish of Kildysart. He has been Principal of Coláiste Ráithín, a second level Gaelscoil in Bray, Co. Wicklow, since 1991.

10 A Day In The Drills

Nora Brennan

IN spring my father made drills with a ruler in his mind and a horse and plough in his hands. By late June rows of leafy green seedlings filled a quarter of The Ash Meadow Field.

When I came home from boarding school there was nothing facing me but crucifying days thinning turnips. Of all the jobs on the farm, thinning was my worst scourge, comparable in my mind to the 'Way of the Cross' and the last agonising hours of Jesus.

To begin with I stripped off all decent clothing. Dressed in a tattered shirt and gathered skirt and carrying sack cloth and binder twine under my arm, I headed for the field. My sister Eileen who had just finished her Leaving Certificate was with me. It was an overcast and humid morning and the lane was cool and damp. Verges were lush and towering stems of foxgloves leaned into our path.

The field tilted south towards the banks of the River Nore. I had little regard for the tranquillity and peace of the place so preoccupied was I with the work on hand. My father had already arrived and was moving steadily along a furrow, like a hedgehog. The turnips were drenched with heavy mist from the night before. My inner cries of protestation about the task ahead had turned to a whimper. There was nothing for it but to wrap the folded sack around my knees and tie one piece of twine above the knee and another below to hold it in place. Soon I was on all fours and off at a crawl. My only hope lay in the fact that the angelus bell would ring out in the valley at noon and within the hour, I would be heading for home. There, I would sit at the right hand of my mother and relish the plateful of boiled bacon, cabbage and new potatoes in front of me.

The sky was beginning to open windows of blue. Wet leaves made for a messy start. My hands were covered in clay and my knees capped with caked earth. The skill I had learned years before came back to me; save the sturdiest looking shoot and clear the rest around it. I carpeted the furrow with bunches of seedlings and leaves as I inched my way forward.

Whenever my father moved ahead with his back to us, my sister and I dawdled. We chatted about her hopes of getting summer work in the nearby hotel – a job that would be easy and pay her better than this. The plan was that another sister, Julia, who already had a summer hotel job, would go for the interview the next day and, if successful, Eileen would turn up for work on the day she was scheduled to begin.

My father had crawled into a new drill and was now facing us. It was time to thin in earnest. My hands were like fine knitting needles darting in and out, reefing handfuls of leaves and leaving single shoots to stand like green stitches cast on brown.

"Ye're doing great work there," he said in his humouring voice as he drew near. "I won't have enough drills to keep ye going at this rate."

"These'll take us three or four days," I said, "and anyway we want to leave some for the others to thin." I was referring to my older brother and sister who were due home the next day for the weekend.

"Well, I'm hoping to be working in the hotel next week,"

Eileen said. "They're looking for summer workers. And they pay well."

"Isn't this better than any hotel job? The finest healthiest work you could get," argued my father back to us. It was a war that we were not going to win.

The morning wore on and the drills grew longer. There was clay and more clay, and leaves. Just then I heard the peal of the bell in the parish church.

My father eyed the sun and studied its position in relation to the vast expanse of countryside that swept from Murphy's field to Hamilton's hill on the western horizon. With the chapel bell at noon and at six o'clock as well as the path of the sun, he rarely drew on the watch in his waistcoat pocket.

"One more drill and then we'll go for dinner," I said.

"Fair enough," he replied.

The sight of my sister removing the sack cloth was enough to get me over the last hurdle. With bags and binder twine discarded on the ditch, we sprinted across the headland and raced each other down the rugged lane. The cool breeze was like a healing balm on my boiling knees.

My father, always eager to get on with a task, didn't dally after dinner but rose quickly and headed back to the field. It was my sister's turn to stay behind and bring tea out in the afternoon. I lingered around as long as possible and then trundled back up the lane.

The sun had burned off any remaining damp leaving the furrows hard and rugged. The drills we had thinned in the morning looked very bare, the single shoots limp and fragile. Those that were pulled lay like green ribbons in the furrows. My hessian bags were already moulded into the shape of my kneecaps and wrapped easily. Dried out lumpy clay ripped my fingers and scalded my knees. Each glance ahead filled me with despair.

On my own, I had little distraction except for the insects. I began to play hide and seek with large black beetles and spiders as they scooted about when I stripped them of shelter.

I had almost turned into a pillar of salt looking around by the time Eileen arrived with the tea. Even my father was showing signs of weariness with his hat thrown back from his forehead as he stood on the headland.

We sat in silence on a few stones by the ditch and ate fresh currant bread which my mother had baked. Tea never tasted so refreshing and sweet.

Looking around the field then, I knew that with all hands on deck the following day, I would survive the agony of the drills for another year.

Nora Brennan grew up on a farm outside Inistioge but now lives in Kilkenny city. A retired teacher, she began creative writing seven years ago and has had several stories and poems published.

11 Majesty Of The Kestrels

Art Ó Súilleabháin

I WAS launching the boats, the beautiful larch, oak and mahogany Corrib clinkers that my Dad had built thirty five years earlier. They had to be launched carefully so as not to scrape the lake-blue finish, and Golden Bay on the north end of the Corrib is a beautiful place to launch and park such gems of woodcraft on the water.

Mrs. Baer who now owns them and the pier where they are stored for her many fishing and picnic trips with family and grandchildren, loves to see them floating and prepared when she arrives for the late season daddy-long-legs fishing in July or August. And the boats are a part of that nature, they need to be in the water for a week or more before the larch swells to close the open joints of wintering in a boat shed.

So it was late June when I was launching the clinkers. I heard a screech overhead but didn't pay much attention. The screeching increased in volume and intensity and I left the boats floating in the small quay to look up into the skies.

I was privileged to be the sole witness to a natural drama that I will probably never witness again. It was a spectacular science of aerobatics performed by three agile and ingenious kestrels. One I presumed to be a male or a female adult was the one conducting the whole exercise.

There was another as a type of onlooker or guiding mentor and the third was definitely a young kestrel being educated in the vital competences of predatory endurance and being encouraged to develop flight skills that would be necessary for survival once it had 'flown the coop'.

The adult kestrel flew to a great height in the sky and having reached this particular zenith it would let something fall from its talons. The screeching of the one waiting below called the juvenile to come streaking from a nearby wood and catch the falling object in its own talons, in mid-flight.

As I watched, it missed once and the other adult flew to where the object landed and proceeded to soar skywards with it again to repeat the procedure. I made out the object to be a small mouse or vole. The lesson was repeated with the mouse being dropped from on high for the juvenile to catch again in mid-flight. Once the lesson had been successfully repeated twice the sky went silent and the three kestrels returned to the cover of the nearby forest of tall conifers.

I stood silently watching for a while, in case I was treated to a repeat performance but that was it. I was stunned by the fantastic and incredible images that were indelibly etched on my memory. I could only marvel at the natural ingenuity, at the elemental flight training exercise and at the whole awesome creativity of it all.

I had been a solitary witness to one of nature's most captivating moments. I didn't photograph it, I didn't video it, it will not appear on my Facebook page or go 'viral' on YouTube for the world to enjoy.

But I witnessed it. It is my personal memory that can only be recalled and recounted in words. It would only happen because I was out in the natural world, moving between water and sky, treasuring a moment of now-ness that can never again be repeated.

Then I was gifted a moment by nature. It is one of the many wonderful moments that have been gifted to me by this elemental paradise of Corrib, moments that never cease to amaze me.

Art Ó Súilleabháin comes from Corr na Móna in Co. Galway, on the shores of Lough Corrib. He is a recently retired former Director of Mayo Education Centre and has six children. Art has written a number of books for children.

12 Milk Cheque Joy

Christopher Moore

IT is 10 o'clock on a hot summer morning in July 1959 and my father walks in from the milking. He has a relaxed look on his face. He carefully removes a long brown envelope and hands it to my mother, unopened.

The eagerly awaited milk cheque has finally arrived and not a moment too soon. It has come with the morning newspaper in one of the three empty 12 gallon milk churns that have been swapped by Merville Dairies lorry man, Christy Brogan.

Christy has taken our three full churns of milk at sunrise. The full churns are wheeled out each night after the rosary and just before bedtime to the elevated stand on the front wall of the garden.

Mercifully, none of yesterday's milk has been returned because of souring, a real bonus in this hot summer weather. This is mainly due to the care and attention my mother has lavished on the dairy throughout the unusual hot spell.

She has changed the cooling water in which the churns rest at least three times during the day. She takes the cheque in her hands, looks at it carefully, tenderly even. She then stuffs it in the pocket of her wraparound navy apron with the tiny white spots.

She looks a bit weary; perhaps it is the sultry weather.

I don't think my mother sees the majestic trees, the wide green pastures or the serene, gentle rolling landscape that stretches before her all the way to Bellewstown Hill in the North or the Carnes to the West.

She has her children, her chores and her thoughts and a well-smoked cigarette in the corner of her mouth. There is at least an inch of ash just about to collapse from its smoked end. This is her usual posture. My siblings wonder if and when the ash will collapse into the sink. My mother, however, is a kind of magician and always manages to prevent what seems to us the inevitable.

Dad is having an egg and a bit of buttered toast and drinking a cup of hot sweet tea while steadily devouring the Irish Independent. This is part of his morning routine. His day begins early, a quick cup of tea, the milking of our 15 cows and the feeding of the calves and then the late leisurely breakfast.

Today he is happy and to my mind greatly relieved. He has handed over responsibility for the money to my mother as he invariably does and he can now properly unwind.

Mother turns to me and says: "Christy, will you ever run down to Howards and get me a half stone of flour and two lbs of sultanas. I want to make a few scones for the tea and tell Mrs. Howard to send up the bill when she is ready."

My father adds: "While you are at it would you get me two ounces of walnut plug and a couple of boxes of matches, like a good lad".

She gives me the shopping bag and squeezes a many sided three-penny bit into my hand. The coin feels solid and substantial. It sits comfortably in the right-hand pocket of my brown corduroy trousers. "Get yourself a few sweets but remember to keep some for your brothers and sisters."

I trot off down the road past our front garden. A grey squirrel that had been harvesting in the near paddock jumps effortlessly from the grass onto the base of the tree and glides upwards like quicksilver at my approach.

Today all is peaceful and I can see the parent hares' ears like flattened fingers protruding from a tuft of rank grass and bright yellow buttercups about 20 yards from the road, so I continue on my way knowing all is well. Just before the entrance to Howard's shop there is a small paddock on the left of the road, filled with birch and briar and low derelict mud walls.

Mrs. Howard's yard is a square grey-stone covered space enclosed by cow-byres and other buildings. It faces south and is a real sun trap. I am particularly vigilant to give Howard's old sheepdog, Captain, a wide berth. Captain is old and deaf and does not like to be woken suddenly, particularly when the sun is shining and he is way down in his dreams. He has previously given me a severe bite just above the right ankle. While Captain lies asleep, basking in the warm summer sunlight there is no sign of my friends Paudge and Peter Howard. They are probably helping their dad at the hay. I knock on the door and Mrs Howard comes out with a large dark shiny key to open the shop.

The shop is a wonder. You can buy paraffin there, which she takes from a barrel outside. For this purpose she uses a very large green tin jug with a round snout angled upwards at about 45 degrees. She keeps the jug in the shop so the paraffin smell mingles with the smell of the flour and the raisins and the tobacco till I struggle to segregate the smells in my mind and I forget what it is I came for, but Mrs Howard knows.

Her milk cheque has also come today and she can guess, more or less, what I will need. "I suppose your mammy needs flour, she says before I return to the real world, and maybe your daddy needs tobacco".

I nod affirmatively.

Concentration has returned momentarily but quickly evaporates as I see the jars of brightly coloured sweets on top of the counter. The dark red aniseed balls, black and white bull's-eyes, light green and white rock, toffees, multicoloured gobstoppers and even chocolate whisper to me. I am sure Mrs Howard must think I am some sort of imbecile but she probably knows that it is tough being 10 years old with only three pence in your pocket when important decisions have to be made.

I am not always faced with this dilemma. Usually when I come to the shop I have my list but no money in my pocket and I can only look and drool at the wonderful selection of goodies. But today I am prosperous. The milk cheque has come and for the next week or so I may have further delicious decisions to make, I can only hope.

With that I leave the shop and Mrs Howard locks up. I have nearly forgotten to ask for the bill. "Mammy wants you to make up our bill, Mrs Howard," I say.

"I'll have it in a few days", she replies.

I leave the shop; walk out of the yard and up the road towards home. When I get to the bent chestnut tree Sparks, our white Jack Russell terrier, comes yapping and barking and jumping to meet me. He circles me several times making me swallow the last of the aniseed ball that I had only been licking since I left the shop. This is bad news indeed as I am forced to take another one from the packet

I crush the remains of the aniseed ball and swallow it quickly. I lick my lips to remove the residue of the coloured sweet from around my mouth. Then I go in, my father is dying for a bit of fresh tobacco, the last of his supply had gone yesterday before the cheque had arrived. Had his lack of tobacco coincided with Sunday he would have put it on Mrs Howard's bill.

My mother is now sitting down drinking tea, her cigarette long since extinguished; she inspects the flour and sultanas and indicates that we will have scones for tea.

When my sisters and brothers arrive the sweets are divided and everybody is reasonably satisfied but my younger brother Peter has suspicions concerning the fact that there are only ten aniseed balls left. At this point I give him an extra sweet and as usual the bribe works and he start chewing and forgets about the missing aniseed balls.

My father finishes his pipe and decides that he will go to the field to inspect the potatoes and to dig some for today's dinner and for the dinner for the next few days. I volunteer to go with him; I love the smell of the freshly dug potatoes as they are lifted from the soil on a warm sunny day. We cross the fields accompanied by Sparks and also Fido our large Collie dog.

When we arrive back from the digging, mother is rolling out pastry for the scones. An air of calm and contentment has descended on the household.

The milk cheque has arrived today and mammy is making scones for the tea. For this week at least we are in heaven.

Christopher Moore is retired member of the Defence Forces and lives in Stamullen, Co Meath. Married with four adult children and seven grandchildren, his hobbies include gardening and writing.

13 Cows At The Cliffside

Michael Flahive

IN the late 50s and early 60s, three or four times in the summer, the cows were left into the promontory fort in Bromore in Kerry to graze in the daytime. At night between milkings they were kept in the Well Field near the house.

While there for a few days they had to be watched as the fencing was only thorny (barbed) wire on makeshift posts.

If the cows were startled by fox, dog or people from the landside they had only one way to escape and that was over a sheer 180-foot cliff. They were also partial to the sweet grass on the clifftop and the Kerry cows in particular were agile and devious enough to try and avail of it.

Myself and my dog, Faoilean, were usually 'volunteered' to mind the herd while they were there.

Faoilean, the Irish for cliff bird or seagull, got his name because he was black on top and white underneath like the big seagulls that followed the horse and plough in the garden.

I loved the job as the cows were let in to the fort when it was reasonably fine and it was better than the bog or thinning turnips or mangolds. All I had to do was make sure I had the same number in the evening as I had in the morning and report any cow off form, lame or bulling (in heat).

Faoilean and I had our breakfast while the last of the cows were being hand milked and then we set off on our adventure. Faoilean steered the cows out the gap and along the lane to the cliffs. I had a message bag with provisions for the day, it could be soda or griddle bread and homemade butter or cold boiled new potatoes with a pinch of salt and tea or milk in a lemonade bottle and of course a book to pass the time.

When we got them to the promontory fort I pulled in the wooden gate behind them and now we could take it easy as they were going to be busy grazing for a while.

Faoilean and I spent hours watching the ocean and the wildlife, the sea-pigs (dolphins) jumping out of the sea after salmon, the seagulls and fulmars gliding past at eye level and now and again the Blue Hawk – the Peregrine Falcon – sitting on top of 'The Devil's Castle,' a 120 foot high sea stack.

Faoilean only took notice of the grey seals below in Bromore Bay, probably because they had a head like a dog.

We watched the fishing boats from the Cashen south of Ballybunion or the Clare boats from Kilbaha or Carrigaholt tending their lobster pots under Bromore Cliffs. We saw the cargo ships steaming in and out through the Shannon Estuary. Sometimes I would tell Faoilean their names if I could make them out with the old brass spyglass or telescope.

We didn't neglect our job and Faoilean gave a low growl if one of the cows went too close to the wire. Usually when they had enough grazed they lay down and chewed the cud. This was our chance to check the nearby strands from 180 foot above and if anything – a rope, a net or timber was washed in my Aunty Peg would come and mind the cows while my brothers and I would climb down the narrow steep track to the strand to collect whatever bounty was there. Aunty Peg's only condition was that we also bring up some periwinkles, sea-grass (duilisc), carrageen or sluachan.

The sea-grass was dried in the sun on a corrugated iron

roof and kept in a brown paper bag for occasional use. The periwinkles were cooked that day and eaten by all in the house that night. We would pick the cap off the shell with a needle or safety pin and extract them slowly with the pin so as to get the full length of them, simple but delicious.

I would save some for the cliffs the following day. I tried to introduce Faoilean to periwinkles but he was not impressed, he preferred sea-grass.

I also tried the scurvy grass that colonised one small section of the fort, it had a carpet of lovely scented white flowers but the taste was not as pleasant, the bitterness lingered long after it was spat out. I sometimes ate raw sorrel with the cold potatoes; it had a nice tangy flavour. We had a plentiful supply of cool spring water from the small well on the side of cliff at the fort-Tobaireen na Si (the Fairies Little Well), there was always an enamel mug hidden in the grass nearby which we shared, Faoilean did not mind.

The grass at Bromore Fort was cliff-grass, salt and wind resistant and as it was only grazed a few times a year it developed an overgrown mat underneath that had a distinctive earthy scent when the cows pulled tufts of it.

'Saltwaters', nowadays called tourists, hikers or trekkers asked if they could take our picture, Faoilean would give a short bark and look at me for instructions. One said we were 'quaint' and gave me a half a crown not realising I knew the meaning of both.

Another couple from 'the States' asked did I go to school and out of pure devilment I said: "No". I can still see the look of sadness and pity on their faces, if they could they would have adopted the "two pups" there and then. Well it was the summer holidays so I was not exactly lying.

If the weather changed and got wet or cold we had the

refuge of the "Soldiers Camp", a disused look-out post (LOP) from the Second World War.

The LOP on Bromore Fort was one of four guarding the Mouth of the Shannon, the other three were at Kerry Head, Loop Head and Kilcredaun in Co. Clare. It was a concrete flat roofed structure with a door, six windows to seaward and a fireplace and chimney. When the war ended in 1945 the LOP was abandoned.

We used it as shelter and there was always a bag of turf and a few cipins to light a fire. Faoilean could sit up on the old table there not under it as at home. He had a great view of the cows out of the windows and I would sit on the sugawn chair reading. I read several chapters of "The Coral Island" to him and he understood every word.

There was a map painted on the wall near the door, it was of the local area out to Kerry Head and across to Loop Head in Clare. I learned the villages and headlands-Meenoghane, Clashmealcon, Kilbaha, Leck Point and Kilstiffin – The Enchanted Ground- a mythical lost island in the sea under Rehy Hill. I did not need to go to school.

As I got older my father got a battery electric fence, a big green round one on a spike that was pushed into the ground. Within days the Kerry cows, me and Faoilean discovered the power of it.

There was no longer a need to mind the cows continuously at the cliffs and I was more use in the garden, the bog or the meadows. It was the end of an era – the last days of minding the cows at the cliffs.

Mike Flahive farms a mile north of Ballybunion in Co Kerry. Married with two children, his family opened Bromore Cliffs as a tourist attraction three years ago.

14 The Big Chill Of 1947

Daniel Kearns

AS a young boy growing up on a farm in north Mayo a few miles west of Crossmolina in the village of Carrowkilleen, I shiver still at the recall of the great blizzard of 1947.

The first snow fell on Monday the 24th of February. On the following day it developed into a full-blown snowstorm, considered the worst in living memory. It isolated the West and stopped all industry and the Shannon Electricity system failed in the North West cutting off all power and light. The telephone system also failed. People believed it to be the worst natural catastrophe since the night of the big wind, Sunday the 6th of January 1839 when it is said over 70 people were killed or drowned.

I remember the snow falling heavily and being driven by a very cold easterly wind that would freeze the nose and other parts off a brass monkey. It blew the snow into great drifts 10/15ft deep especially against buildings and homes.

With my father and brother we brought our sheep into the haggard for food and safety and it was a dreadful task as you could only see a very short distance as roads and landmarks were disappearing quickly under the massive snowfall.

Afterwards we considered ourselves very lucky as only a couple of miles away three men perished that night in the blizzard. Two were the MacAndrew brothers, then in their seventies, who had lived all their lives together. One went out for a bag of turf and when he didn't return the other brother went to look for him, saw him in a drain, tried to pull him out and both were found there the next day frozen to death. They had to be brought down the mountain on two doors supported by shovel handles. A priest from Corrick and friends walked the long distance in deep snow to administer the last rites.

Nearby Patrick Rowland (26) went to tend a sick animal but lost his way and was found like his two neighbours the following day. Fr Brady walked three miles from Keenagh, this time bare-foot in the snow and back to also administer last rites.

On Wednesday the 26th most homes and buildings were covered in snow. We had to cut corridors through it to reach the haggard, animal buildings and turf stack. Only the chimney smoke indicated the location of some homesteads. A giant snowman was carved out of a huge drift in the front garden.

The harvest of '46 was a terrible one that in ordinary circumstances would be bad enough; now with most of the fodder used up the problems were only beginning. Prices of hay and corn shot up and the other problem was to find a supplier.

We had a fine stack of turf that meant a big open fire where all the cooking and pot boiling was carried out hung from a large crane over the fire. We had our own supply of potatoes, veg, fresh eggs, milk and butter. A small river passed by our house and a nearby spring well supplied the drinking and tea making water.

People in towns were affected far worse than us as they had become accustomed to the power. We had a dry/wet battery radio that kept us in touch with the outside world.

One of the worst hit industries was the Western People

newspaper that required the power to keep its linotype machines going. However it did manage to get some issues printed and one arrived in Westport and was passed around till all the print left its pages. Buses were caught in drifts and the mail car was lost between Ballina and Belmullet. Local people looked after those people wherever they found them.

Farmers, especially the mountain folk, suffered great animal losses that were only truly discovered as the snow melted.

Birds suffered terribly and robins and other birds came into our kitchen for warmth and food where they were well looked after. Hares, grouse, snipe and plover also fared badly on account of the frozen ground. The grouse never fully recovered as their basic diet, the heather, was snow-covered for a long time and then with the advent of forestry planting most of their natural habitat was done away with forever.

Finally, the big thaw set in and the snow disappeared as did our giant snowman. The ice melted on our Lough that brought so much joy and happiness to the youngsters at a time when our elders had to endure such great hardship.

Spring gradually unfolded before finally blossoming into full growth when again the lands were tilled and sown. The lambs played in the fields, farmyard fowl hatched out their broods, the birds sang from the tree tops, the man snipe dived through the evening skies making that lovely drumming sound, a rare sound today.

Even the odd grouse call could be heard from the distant moorland. The larks ascended and descended from the clear blue skies singing their songs of praise. The hay was saved, the corn was harvested and the hum of the thresher drum could be heard from a neighbour's holding in the distance, heralding its approach to the next haggard, ensuring big straw stacks and full granaries.

Life went on...

Daniel Kearns is a native of Carrowkilleen, Crossmolina, Co Mayo and is a former county council official. Married with three grown-up children and three grand children, he now writes as a hobby.

15 The 'White Face'

Seán Hallinan

'**D**ID you see that... did you see it?"

Frank's voice was grave and deeply in earnest. I could see the trauma in his face as he manoeuvred the boat's engine. The Mayfly season had arrived and we were on Lough Carra. A fresh westerly wind tossed, turned and moulded a multifaceted wave. We had drifted out from the point of Derrinrush. It was a favoured dark ribbon of water along an underwater shelf between the shallows and deeper water.

"A great spot for a wild Carra trout to be hanging out," Frank assured me. We had, however, caught a fleeting glimpse of a creature that most definitely was not a trout.

Franks voice was troubled as he pressed me further: "It was really big... did you not spot it?

"Ah, I just heard a splash and from the corner of my eye I saw the sun reflecting on its shiny back... maybe it was an otter or a giant pike?" I ventured.

He was highly dismissive of the idea. "That was no otter... that was no monster pike... it was much bigger." Then in a voice barely audible he said: "That was the White Face."

I did not like to probe further as I could see he was distressed. Silence reigned. Frank reeled in his flies, Murragh, Green Peter and Mayfly and put them back in the case. I held my dapping rod aloft with hook on the first ring as we wove our way through a well-worn path in the reeds towards the boat berths on the shore.

Frank spoke very little on the way home and words were still scarce as we tucked into tea at his house.

It had been a strange afternoon and there had been odd omens on the Lough from the first drift. A bedraggled crow flying southward had been snatched and carried off in the claws of a hunting hawk. A lone black cormorant stood like a sentry on a group of rocks and quite unusually did not take flight as we trolled by.

A flock of gulls had suddenly swooped close to the boat devouring any airborne flies and they let out piercing squawks as they dived low and gorged on the spent gnats drifting on the waters. We cursed them.

In the following days Frank never spoke of what we had observed and I did not expect him to. I knew that momentary vision he had on the dark waters of the lake had a deep personal affect on him.

He had an intimate knowledge of the lake. Beyond the twin Islands, out by Moore's Island or the Hag were favoured fishing spots that had often yielded splendid wild Carra trout. In winter with dog and gun he had hunted its shores for duck, wild goose and woodcock. Frank's fame had spread far and wide around Carra as a champion "pike man."

With fork or grape clutched in his fist he could run, skid, swivel and slide to gain advantage over monster pike he had viewed beneath the ice. The custom and tradition had been handed on from father to son down the generations. In lean years when hunger had never been far from a country man's door, a monster pike sustained a family for a fortnight or more.

Frank told me how 1963 was a legendary year in the

annals of hunting the pike on Carra. From mid-December the country was held in the unrelenting grasp of a bitter cold Siberian wind. The accompanying frost set in early in the afternoons and penetrated every living thing. Cattle lowed in the fields hungry for fodder. Crosscuts and chain saws swung into action as men felled trees for precious firewood to keep their families warm. The work was often dispensed with as others made haste to the Carra to enjoy the piking, morning and evening. Men, old and young from the surrounding communities, congregated on the frozen bays and inlets around the lake.

First they patrolled the deep out yonder. Parties of five or six abreast stretched across the bay, drumming the ice in order to hunt the great pike towards the shallows by the shore. Sometimes the fish bolted and made a desperate dash for the deep. Men whooped with excitement as they slid across the ice to cut them off.

Many times, the hunters were successful and turned the fish. On other occasions, the chase was in vain as the pike broke the gauntlet and disappeared into the deep.

Often the ice tapping with fork handle and due diligence to the task ensured a great fish was ushered into shallow waters. When he was clearly visible underneath the ice – his great gills expanding and contracting from exhaustion – the sledgehammer was called into play. Ten massive hits ensured a large hole was broken in the ice. Often the fish moved a few paces further forward and the process had to be repeated a number of times.

Then inevitably there came the final surrender. The fish was pinned with one fork and whipped clear in one great swoop by another. There were great cries of joy as the skilful task was accomplished. Time old tradition was honoured as the "first spotter" always claimed and received the fish.

Rarely if ever was there any danger to the pike men. They respected the waters and always knew when the ice was strong enough to sustain a party of pike men. On one occasion that year, a brazen fellow sank through a spring hole in the ice. Vigilant comrades had a rope at the ready and he was hauled to safety.

Many years later I was musing on those distant days with the son of Frank, the 'Pikeman of Carra'. I related our strange experience on the waters out from the point of Derrinrush.

"I know what that was about," he assured me. "It stemmed from a springtime when we were ploughing and cultivating the land. My father was working with a mare 'Katie' who laboured on lands at Kilfaul and Moorehall. She was a family friend and a great grafter that could pull any load.

"A beautiful shapely chestnut beast, she had a distinctive white face. I was but a boy and one morning he sent me to Derrinrush to halter her. She had been grazing on the sedge by the shore. I had the head-collar but there was no chance of catching her. She was standing rigid, wooden-like and frozen facing the Lough. I could not put on the halter as her head and neck were stone stiff and I could not reach up.

"I raced home to fetch my father. When we returned there wasn't a trace of 'Katie' on the shore. Out yonder she was disappearing into the deep, with just a glimpse of a hind quarter sinking slowly. There was neither sight nor sound of 'Katie' from that day.

"It had a great affect on my father and on occasions when he lamented his loss, it preyed on his mind so much that he could no longer bear to look on the Lough."

Seán Hallinan works in the Museum of Country Life, Turlough Park, Castlebar, Co Mayo. In his early sixties, he is the current chairperson of Baile an Tobair GAA. He has dedicated this story to the memory of his late father-in-law – Frank McDonnell R.I.P of Moorehall – "The Pike-man of Carra".

16 The Night Liston KO'd Patterson – And My Mother

Meta Waters

RURAL Ireland of the 1950s was a far cry from what we know of it today. Very few families had cars and bicycles were in great use. Neighbours 'rambled' at night visiting other houses and catching up on the local news.

Farm life only changed slowly in the previous three decades, the tractor had begun to replace the horse-drawn plough but other aspects of life remained relatively unchanged. Cows were milked by hand, hay saved into reeks and corn threshed using the threshing machine.

It was into one such farm that I was born in the late 1950s, the youngest of four children with three older brothers. Our farming method was mixed, but that was the norm in those days. We had dairy cows, sheep, a few pigs for our own supply of ham and bacon, hens, corn crops, forage crops and a corn mill.

Money was scarce except when cattle were sold or when there was a good harvest. As in most farming households, the woman of the house supplemented the income by keeping hens and selling the eggs and also in our case, by making butter.

Every Wednesday she churned the milk producing delicious 'country butter' and sold it on Fridays on her weekly visit to the town. This gave her a good income and indeed we were often glad of it to provide clothing and shoes for the family in bad years.

Week in, week out the butter was made and it was only on a very few occasions that she was unable to supply her customers – a couple of weeks around the time her children were born.

However, there was another occasion in September 1962 when Sonny Liston knocked out Floyd Patterson in the World Heavyweight Championship – an occasion which left my mother groggy as well.

That time was still before Telefís Éireann was up and running and television sets were few and far between in rural Ireland. BBC television could be received by erecting a very high aerial and my father did that on top of the corn mill. Our house was a well-known rambling house and it was common for family and neighbours to gather for big television moments and for big fights.

My mother laid out spare mattresses in the loft for those coming to watch the fight. It took place in the early hours – Irish time – so the plan was for a number of neighbours to go to bed for a few hours in our house and my father would rouse them in time for the first round. All went to plan, at first, with several neighbours arriving after their work, some on foot, some on bicycles and even one on his little Ford tractor.

There was a jovial atmosphere as we served up cups of tea and homemade bread and cakes. As the evening wore on and it was still too early for bed, my father produced a bottle of poitín that he was saving for such an occasion. Of course, this was no ordinary poitín, it was 'one of me specials' as 'Francie the Still' would call it.

Francie lived on the edge of the bog, some three to four miles away, and was known for the quality of his illicit produce. He could distil the requirements for the whole locality in any given year. Everyone knew it was illegal but sure weren't we providing the man with a few bob in those hard times. Before long a right session of singing and storytelling was under way and even my mother, who seldom imbibed, joined in.

Around midnight, with the poitín bottle empty, all the revellers went to whatever bed had been allocated to them with my father promising to call them in time for the fight.

Televisions then were not as sophisticated as they are today. After switching on the set it took several minutes for it to warm up and produce a picture. This meant my father was up about a quarter of an hour before the fight to have the television running properly and to call all the interested parties. However, he had not anticipated the job that would be. Many of them were unaccustomed to drinking spirits and were almost comatose when he tried to rouse them.

Having woken the last one, dad went back down stairs to watch the fight. He got the shock of his life when he looked at the television set to discover that the action was already over. Liston had knocked out Patterson after just two minutes of the first round and my father had missed the entire fight.

By the time they all filed back to bed another hour had gone by and it was a very quiet household the next morning with nobody stirring until well after dawn.

It was churning day too but, for once, my mother was nowhere to be seen. In fact she did not appear in the kitchen until close to 11 o'clock. She claimed that she was up half the night with all the racket going on downstairs. Behind her back, my father just winked at us and smiled. Years later she confessed that she had drunk a little too much and suffered the consequences.

And so it was on that on her weekly rounds of her customers in the town she had to repeat over and over "No butter today."

Sonny Liston had knocked out Floyd Patterson and my mother suffered a technical KO on the night too.

Meta Waters is from Aharney, Tullamore, Co Offaly and was brought up in nearby Durrow. Married with two grown-up sons, she is a local government official and enjoys story-telling.

17 The First Ploughing Day Of Spring

Mark McGaugh

BY the time I left Ireland for foreign shores, the tractor was gradually replacing the horse as the preferred method of ploughing as well as carrying out lots of other farm related work.

However we never had a tractor on our land before my departure in January, 1960. My memory is of time spent with the horse ploughing, harrowing, drilling, and scuffling the beet. We were part of a team with the horse playing the leading role, and a working relationship was established which was based on trust, kindness, and the will and desire to finish the job in hand.

Particularly crystalised in my memory is the first ploughing day of spring. I picture the cold morning air when the horses are taken from the stables and they almost appear to be looking forward to the day's work ahead. They are alert and frisky with their heads held high and the sparkle on their coats suggests that they are eagerly awaiting the task of ploughing the land.

There was an age difference in the two horses; Fanny barely two years had old, had only been broken in the previous autumn, while Blackie was an experienced six-year-old who had done every job expected of him on the farm. These tasks included pulling the common and spring harrow once the field was ploughed, the smaller plough for drilling the field where the various seeds would be sown at a later date. The horse was busy throughout the spring and summer and into the autumn as they were the driving force for the heavy work carried out on the farm.

The old Pearce plough was prepared, with both wheels being oiled, the crosschecked, with a touch of paint on the implement to spruce it up for another year's duty.

The horses too needed preparations. We had a blacksmith named John Molloy in the village who had carried on the traditions of his father and grandfather before him of turning long metal rods of iron into properly fitting shoes for horses in our locality.

The aroma still lingers of the moment when the Smithy first tested the red-hot steel to the horse's hooves to ascertain if it was a correct fitting. Those steel shoes were essential for the animals to get a grip in the earth as they trudged along turning the deep heavy soil onto its side.

The ploughing was normally done in co-operation with another relative or more often with a neighbour as very few farmers had more than one horse, and two horses were needed to pull the heavy plough. On the first day of ploughing the gear was loaded on to the horse-cart and taken to the two-acre field, with one horse travelling along behind the cart.

There was always a sense of excitement about that day, as well as a little trepidation in case there might be problems with the plough. In land freshly reclaimed, there were likely to be stubborn stones or tree roots, which could easily result in the cross of the plough being broken.

As the first furrows were being created by the brown earth covering the previous year's field of oats, both my brothers were already working in unison, with Tom holding the reins and guiding Fanny and Blackie to keep a straight line to the headland while Eamon expertly steered the handles of the plough.

It did not take long for the crows, blackbirds, and seagulls to realise that a ready-made meal was being made available on the blackened soil to them, and their newly hatched chicks nestling in the trees and the lakeshore a short distance away.

To the amateur onlooker the process of ploughing appeared to be simple, but there had to be some technical preparation beforehand, as the headland area needed to be measured out in order to give the turning space to the horses at the end of each furrow. The positioning of the two wheels of the plough determined the depth of the furrow, and the depth was influenced by the crops – sugar beet, or potatoes both required deeper soil, while turnips could thrive on a comparatively shallow drill.

Ploughing in particular was not measured by the clock but by the amount of daylight available; yet it was essential the horses and the workers also had a proper lunchtime break. We took our responsibility very serious for the welfare of the horses, and made sure there was a supply of oats and water available for them at lunchtime. The horses were eager for their lunch treat as the bags of oats were hung over their head, which they consumed with real relish.

There was always an afternoon break as well so that the work continued until the sun cast long shadows through the woodlands surrounding Lough Corrib, before disappearing behind the Twelve Pins on the Connemara Mountains.

By then, Tom and Eamon were jaded as they wiped their furrowed brows after the strains of a long day's toil. The physical exertions were visible as the perspiration trickled down their unshaven faces. However, there was also an overwhelming feeling of joy in seeing the result of their work from the changed colour of the tilled field, knowing that they would be back to finish the job off on the morrow.

When Thomas Gray wrote the 'Elegy Written in a Country Churchyard' his opening stanza portrays the story of 'The Ploughman' in not just a poetic manner, but it also encapsulates the very essence of farming as I remember it in the middle of the last century.

'The curfew tolls the knell of parting days, the
lowing herd winds slowly over the lea,
The Ploughman homewards plods his weary way,
and leaves the world to darkness and to me.'

Mark McGaugh is a native of Shrule, Co Mayo but emigrated in 1960. Married with three grown up children and five grandchildren, he retired from business after 40 years and now enjoys writing.

18 Scythe Man

Declan P. Gowran

NED took the long slasher and the bow-saw from the outhouse to cut and chop the windfall wood down on Tom Byrne's farm off the road to Graney. He did chores for his neighbour, who was retired, like cutting hay and mending fences. In return Ned was allowed to use some of the facilities on the farm like the stable where he kept his brown pony 'Lady' and his two-wheeled red and blue farm cart. Ned fetched Lady from the field and fixed the halter and reins to lead her on.

Ned was a tall man who always wore a brown fedora hat stained from the sweat of labour. He wore a check shirt and a necktie under a grubby waistcoat that held his briar pipe, tobacco and pocket watch. For trousers he favoured brown corduroys with braces, and for footwear hob-nailed boots. My big brother Jimmy and I used to stay with him and his wife Cathleen in Carrigeen Cottage near the Pike at Carrigeen Crossroads for the summer holidays.

"Who wants to be first?" Ned asked in his whistling voice.

Jimmy and I looked at each other unsure of what Ned meant, pondering a right response.

"Who wants to be the first to ride 'Lady'?"

"I do," we both cried out, jumping up and down and holding up our hands like when we were asked an easy question in the classroom. Ned decided to toss a coin and I won. I was chuffed. My brother was disconsolate.

"Sure you can ride her home, Jimmy," Ned consoled him with a pat on his head.

Jimmy bucked up then as Ned lifted me bodily on to the pony's curved back.

"Hold the reins firmly, but loosely," he instructed me. "Grip her by the flanks and tuck in with your legs. Sit straight up and follow her movements up and down as if you were a part of her."

I did as Ned said, a little nervously, but thrilled at the same time. It was amazing: riding bareback like a Red Indian. "Giddy-up!" I called out to encourage her, and just as quick I felt myself slipping to one side off-balance. Instinctively I made a grab for the pony's mane. Ned saved me with a muscular arm and held me in position as I settled back. Somehow I managed to stay aboard, bouncing up and down like a piston, my thighs rubbing the carpet of her hair, tickling me.

Ned chopped the fallen branches into firewood, sculpting outrageous shapes, and we helped to gather it into the cart which he had hitched up to 'Lady' with practised precision for transporting back to Carrigeen Cottage. As we neared completion of our task, and prepared to haul the load home, Tom Byrne came hobbling up the lane. A wizened old man, he wore a baggy grey suit that once obviously fitted a larger frame. He stopped and tapped an odd clump of dock-weed with his walking stick.

"God bless the work," he declared by way of a greeting. He doffed his tweed cap: "But will ye not come in for a pick-me-up afore ye go, will ye now?"

We did. Ned and himself imbibed of the best poteen countrywide while my brother and I drank our ginger ale. When Ned stood up it was with a promise that we would be back the following morning to cut the meadow at the back of Tom's thatched farmhouse.

The air was hot and dry that morning, alive with the hum of insects as he fetched the scythe from the barn. Slowly, deliberately, neatly, he rolled up the sleeves of his shirt, sans collar.

He lifted his fedora briefly to wipe his brow with his 'kerchief. He then held the angled stock of the scythe firmly upright against his body, the great shiny blade arcing away from him like the crescent of the moon.

With slow methodical strokes he caressed the razor edge with the sharpening stone singing and rasping, pausing now and then to moisten it with a spit. He grasped the skewish handgrips of the scythe, described a few practice swings before wading into the sea of lush green grass that shivered to the music of the imperceptible breeze.

He swung the scythe deliberately, like a pendulum: back and forth, back and forth in mini-hemispheres. The blades of grass collapsed silently from the stroke of the cut to lie gently in wreath ranks, criss-crossing the field. Mechanically he swathed through the mid-height lawn with nothing but the sound of the bite of the blade against brittle stems, guillotining the grass, and the odd startled squawk of a bird to disturb his composure.

All around the border of the field the ash trees trembled. Now and then frantic insects interloped in a love dance with the wildflowers; buzzing like bees, crackling like a grasshopper or silently like a butterfly, fluttering on the wing. Ned would pause with regularity to mop his brow and to cast a backward glance and survey the extent and progress of his work. As the grass fell the perfume began to rise and dissipate. The scent was barely noticeable in the nostril at first, but soon it drowned the air with its sweet, overpowering narcosis.

The sun was burning hot and high in the sky before Ned finished his cutting, his face shining like a tomato from the heat and his muscular exertions swinging the scythe. Gingerly, he walked across the levelled field of hay for a cup of cooling water as the rising release of pollen seemed to have shocked the very oxygen from the air.

He returned in a few days to turn the grass. For this task he used the twin pronged fork. He lifted the grass, and tossed it, and teased it, and twisted it, helping it to dry. In the merciless heat the grass slowly cooked to a crispy brown colour. After a few more days incineration it was time to build the cocks. Fork by fork they were weaved into their traditional shape bound together by the crackled hay. So the haycocks would sit and fructify, baked by the sun and flavoured by the scent of the spent juicy grasses blending together, protected from the rotting rain.

My brother and I helped a little but watched in awe as this man elevated manual farm labour into a poetic form as by cutting lines of grass with a scythe.

Then in the afternoon, the artist would paint this pastoral scene by dotting Tom Byrne's field with drumlins of hay on the yellow stubble.

Declan P Gowran (65) lives in Dublin. Married with four children and two grandsons, he is retired from Dublin Bus as a former driver and Tour Guide. He enjoys gardening, DIY and writing.

19 The Potato Sowers

Moira Gallagher

CREESLOUGH in Donegal was made famous by Percy French's popular song 'The Emigrants Letter' (Cutting the Corn in Creeslough). He composed this song when he was an engineer around the area in 1910.

Less well-known is the fact that Creeslough won the world record in the 1950s for the largest crop of potatoes grown per acre, an impressive 35 tons and six hundredweight. For the local farmers receiving the World Cup was a great achievement and along with it a sense of pride in their own place for all involved, including my own father.

Work in spring always began with the ploughing. Fields for the various crops were chosen, two horses were yoked to the plough and a new year's work was begun. My father steered the plough, cutting straight furrows which made lovely patterns as he sliced open the moist black soil. He was accompanied by flocks of gulls, swooping and screeching waiting to catch worms as the earth was overturned.

Preparations for planting the potatoes saw the seed potatoes being split, ensuring that each cutting had a bud. The splits were placed in wooden boxes with a handle down the middle. Drills were opened, using horses and plough and the farmyard manure was carted to these fields and spread in the drills.

Now it was time for the children to take part. The boxes

of splits were placed at the beginning of each drill and the race was on. The potatoes were planted in a straight line about nine inches apart. We dragged the box along as we worked and everyone tried to be finished first. A careful score was kept of the number of drills one managed to plant each day. My father put some dry fertilizer on top and then closed the drills with the plough. Planting the potatoes was great fun and picnics never tasted so good as those we shared in the potato field.

From planting to harvesting a lot of work had to be done. The grubber tore up the drills and they were hoed for weeds. Then when the tops were touching in the drills the potatoes were moulded. A drill plough pushed the clay up making sure the potatoes were covered. Barrels of spray were prepared using bluestone and washing soda.

My father filled the spraying machine, put it on his back and walked up and down between the drills spraying the stalks and their lovely creamy blossoms to prevent the dreaded blight. This process was repeated every 12 to 14 days, especially if the weather was wet and warm.

When the crop was ready for digging, the seed potatoes that were for sale were sprayed again, or burned, so that they did not get any bigger. Horses and plough were used to slice open the drills. The potatoes were thrown up on either side of the drill. As children, we gathered the loose potatoes while my father and older brothers searched under the clay for those left behind. Potato sacks were filled or sometimes the potatoes were put in large mounds in the field. Each evening these pits were covered with clay to protect them from ground frost. The sacks were carted to an outhouse where they were stored to be sold later.

In the previous century the Third Earl of Leitrim had

constructed a pier at Mulroy to service his estate. Potatoes were exported from the same pier where relatively small cargo boats or coasters would carry the produce of the local farmers to foreign places such as Cyprus, and even as far away as the Solomon Islands in the Pacific Ocean.

It was a simple process – a potato wholesaler informed my father how many tons were required for a certain boat and would give him bags for that amount.

My father had a number template which had to be polished on each bag. Before the bags were filled the potatoes were 'skipped' or sorted on a large table. They had to be a certain size, no large or small ones or those turned green by being exposed to the sunlight. This job was usually done at night time with the help of a few neighbours. A large weighbridge was used to measure out the exact hundredweight. The bags were sewn with a big packing needle and twine.

Now all was ready for the first hurdle; the sealing. A Department of Agriculture potato inspector came to carry out this all important job. He chose bags at random and spilled out the contents. If any flaws were found, he turned down the whole consignment and every bag had to be skipped again. It was a worry until those little red seals were clipped on.

Then a lorry collected the potatoes and they were taken to the store at Mulroy pier to await the boat. Sometimes the boat was delayed and the potatoes were in storage for a few weeks.

This was a very anxious time as there would always be another inspection before the boat was loaded. One diseased potato and your whole quota was turned down. If this happened all the bags had to be skipped again.

There was never a time when the people didn't expel a

collective sigh of relief as that boat sailed away from Mulroy pier because the money derived from potatoes was a very significant part of the annual income.

Nowadays the wheel has come full cirle. There are no more world records for potatoes grown in our local area as the production of this crop has decreased significantly and we now import a certain amount to supplement our home grown potatoes.

On a visit to a local shop there were potatoes from the Solomon Islands that would have derived from the white Aran banners that my father once exported there.

Moira Gallagher is a native of Creeslough, Co Donegal but now lives in Lifford. Married with three children, she is a retired teacher who has immersed herself in writing as a hobby.

20 The Secret Killer

Eileen Ludlow

BEING raised on a farm in rural Cork in the 1950s was a magical time for a child who loved the outdoors and the friendship of animals.

Being a child then was definitely very different to now. The pace of life was much, much slower and our world was very small, no box in the corner to bring world disasters to our fireside, or phones, or iPads, or all the other electronic gadgets that fill our lives today.

There were a few farmyard dwellers that were not my friends, and my imagination did not choose to draw them into my everyday adventures. The geese were part and parcel of most farmyards those days and they were both noisy and nosey. I often heard it said that you would not need a watchdog if you had a good gander.

The farmers wife's in our locality took great pride in their breeding gander and the less fortunate neighbours who had a goose but no gander would get one of the youngsters to take the said goose, legs tied, wings crossed, with a bag over her head to keep her calm (not sure how the goose felt about this "relaxed state" as she was technically in a straitjacket) and if there was a bicycle handy with a basket the designated messenger bundled the poor goose into it to prepare for the romantic outing to meet Mr Gander.

The child without a bicycle had no choice but to tuck this

weighty bird under her oxter and with a half crown in her hot little fist to pay for the mating, trudge off, sometimes through the fields, to visit the farm of the gander.

The child was usually clueless about this ritual and since children should be seen and not heard, there were no questions asked. When the child arrived at the gander's residence, the goose and the money was taken from them and the lucky youngster was taken into the kitchen and given bread and jam or some other treat while waiting for the business to be transacted in the barn.

When that ended, the poor goose was once more trussed up and given back for the return journey home. Occasionally an enterprising child would consider it a terrible waste of a half crown, since they had no idea what the purpose of the journey was for in the first place, and would pocket the money and return home after a suitable time had elapsed.

Such secrets had a habit of coming unstuck when the owners of the goose and the gander met after Mass on the following Sunday. In a situation like that, a child soon learnt back then that crime did not pay.

The gander brought in a small but very welcome income for the woman of the house, who depended on a little extra cash from the poultry in the form of a good breeding gander, the egg money, a breeding Turkey cock, and the turkey money from Christmas.

When I was about nine or 10, I was sent on an errand to my auntie's house. Upon arrival in the yard I was greeted by the squawking and screeching geese led into battle by a very elegant but ferocious gander. My history with geese had not been good and I really dreaded that particular gander. This was not the first time he had made my life a misery, but usually someone would hear the commotion and come to my rescue, or the dogs would herd him off.

This time there was no such back up. Having found myself cornered by him with no escape route, I was petrified and made a grab for the hissing head with both hands and swung him round and round, carried by the momentum of the movement.

I had no Plan B in my head so when I got tired, I just let go and the bird crashed at some pace into the shed wall. The other geese scattered in every direction but the ill-fated gander lay motionless on the ground. Dead.

I was shocked that I had perpetrated such a terrible crime and was even more terrified at the thoughts of how it would bring some unimaginable punishment.

I did what all children do in such circumstances.

I ran.

When I got near home I hid for a while until I gathered my wits. I decided to go for the big lie by casually reporting that there was no one at my auntie's when I called.

It is some 60 years since this gander killing occurred and I've never told a sinner about it – until now.

The next day we all were treated to the horror of what might have happened to Auntie May's fine gander. I heard how he had been bought in Ballincollig, came from good stock, and had cost the enormous sum of 15 shillings and six pence (15/6), and the six pence had been given back as a 'luck penny.' He was the best breeding gander to have come to the locality in years and now that he was gone, there was a mystery surrounding his death.

His replacement was a small grey Chinese gander that was nothing like his big white predecessor. The new master took over his flock and patrolled with a much more placid nature, and seemed to give me a lot more respect than his predecessor.

Maybe he knew that I was a "gander killer".

Eileen Ludlow was born in Farran, Co Cork but has lived for the past 40 years in Co. Meath. Married with three grown-up children and three grandchildren, she is a holistic therapist and enjoys gardening, reading, painting and scribbling down stories from her childhood.

21 Killing The Pig

Mary Buckley

IT was a ritual like no other on the farm – the annual killing of the pig. Being one of a family of seven children, this slaughter was one of the ways where we were self-sufficient when it came to feeding ourselves.

Farm life is full of life and death – a sow would give birth to a litter and then some time later, one particular pig would be earmarked to go into the barrel later in the year.

My father sharpened the big knife in readiness for the slaughter. Then a neighbour or two dropped in to give a hand also sharpening their knives at the whetstone as part of the liturgy. Inside, my mother readied a white enamel basin with a little salt to collect the blood for the homemade black puddings.

My father, neighbours and my older brother went to the piggery and tied a rope around the back legs of the marked pig. Like a prisoner being escorted to the gallows, the unfortunate pig was marched across the farmyard to a tree happened to have branches in the shape of a big Y.

The rope was expertly thrown over this so that the porcine was hauled up. The squealing pig's mouth was roped and held by one of the helpers as my father administered the stabbing to the pig's heart.

As I held the basin underneath the upturned animal, the blood pumped freely into the basin. Part of my job was to plunge my hand into the hot blood and stir it vigorously in case it would curdle. When the pig was bled dry, I ran with the basin to my mother in the kitchen. Seeing how upset I felt at what I'd just witnessed, she praised me for being so brave, saying she could not have done it for love or money.

That was a tough part of rural life to encounter and experience but it was better than what happened the following year.

Sensing the impending doom, that year's chosen pig made a break for freedom as my father tried to stab him. With a supreme effort to hold onto his life, the pig wriggled so much that he managed to loosen the rope so that he got back to the ground. Then as the adults around were caught in momentary paralysis, she bolted down the farmyard with blood spraying from her undercarriage as she ran.

She dived head first into a reek of straw saved for cattle bedding hoping to avoid the chasing posse.

Almost spent by then, she was located by the men and lifted back to the tree and suspended upside down once again so that she could be bled properly to avoid ruining her meat.

However, so much blood was lost in the chase that there were no black puddings that year. After the killing, the pig was put on a table and covered immediately. My mother then sprung into action by pouring boiling water across the carcass to soften the hairs. All available hands were summoned to shave the bristles off while the body was hot.

When that work was completed my father hung the carcass up in an outhouse and slit the pig's belly to collect the innards that could be eaten and discarded the rest.

The heart, liver and kidneys were eaten so they were saved and the small intestine was emptied and washed clean for the homemade puddings. This was carried out in an open stream, as we had no running water in those days.

The pig was left hanging for a few days and then cut up and salted and put into a timber barrel to preserve it. After a few weeks the bacon was taken out and wrapped in newspaper and hung over the open fire where it hardened and cured.

My mother's busy task only began when the pig was dead and hanging. She had to get to work on the innards, frying off the fat where she collected the lard and kept it for frying throughout the following year.

She also washed and turned and cleaned the intestines to make the homemade puddings. Loaves of white bread were bought and my job was to make a big dish of breadcrumbs by hand and into this was mixed pearl barley, onions, spices and of course the blood to make the black puddings.

The mixture was carefully put into the intestines with one hand while holding the intestine open with thumb and forefinger of the other hand.

These puddings were boiled over the open fire in the bastible and one had to be careful not to burst them. As the job was complete they were put hanging on the handle of the floor brush and hayfork resting on the back of our kitchen chairs.

After all the hard work was completed, the children were sent from house to house to share out our meat and puddings with our neighbours and friends.

We did so happy in the knowledge that when another farmyard had a pig killing later in the year, we would be sure of getting our parcel from them.

Mary Buckley is a farm housewife from Rathcoole, Mallow, Co. Cork. Married with 7 children and 4 grandchildren, she enjoys writing as a hobby.

22 A Day In The Life Of A Farm

Vincent Power

AUGUST 9, 1935. The morning was fine and warm. The cows had been milked and the full churns of milk sent to the local creamery at Kilbeg about one mile away. Our father was the second supplier of milk to this creamery when it was first opened many years previously. He was proud of this and was always keen to show the No. 2 book issued by the creamery. Although the creamery is long since closed we still have this little book in our family scrapbook.

"A fine harvest day," my father said. "We'll make a start on the oats crop in the name of God".

This was his big day, a day he had looked forward to for a long time. The ploughing, harrowing, and sowing of the crop had taken place over the winter and early spring. Scarecrows (fir breaga) had been erected in the cornfields in July to prevent birds from scavenging the ripened grain especially where corn was lodged. The harvest had now come and looked promising.

Bills which had piled up with the creamery over the past six months would be paid from this harvest at threshing time. His family of eight, between three and twelve, could now be safely looked after by their mother, fed, clothed and educated. There was newness in his steps and in his heart and I shared it, being the oldest boy in the family. He donned his corduroy jacket reserved for this important occasion. It had plenty of oil stains on it – grain and straws were still in the pockets from last year's harvest. It was indeed the symbol of his life long profession and he was proud of that.

Preparations for the first day of harvest had been going on for a few weeks. The "reaper and binder" machine was taken from its winter barn. This machine was my father's pride. He had bought it for £29.00 some 30 years before – a genuine 'McCormack made in Canada' embossed on its frame. It had served him well over all these years and sometimes the neighbours too.

An overall service was performed to put it into full working order. This included oiling and greasing, repairing canvasses, sharpening blades and knives and making sure there was ample supply of binder twine for binding the sheafs of corn or bundles as we called them. In addition to servicing the machine, it was equally important to check the horse's equipment – 2/3 horses were required to pull the machine.

A saddler was employed for a few days to ensure that the horses had good tackling as well as blinkers, collars, hames and dromochs. So now on this day, my father, the farm hands, myself, the horses and the great reaper and binder had come together as one, to make a start on the oats in the sandpit field.

On this particular occasion my mother did not appear in the farmyard to see the preparations. She normally did so – offering help but today she had a sick girl (my sister Peg) in bed with pneumonia for the past week. The following day was to have been a special day in our school – the schoolmaster was taking a few of us (including Peg) on an outing to Tramore as we hadn't missed a day at school over the past year. Peg unfortunately was unable to make it. Still this harvest day was bright and promising.

The headland in the cornfield had already been cleared by the farm workers. This process involved clearing a six feet wide path around the perimeter of the field with scythes and was certainly a laborious task on a hot day. The field was now ready for the reaper and binder to commence its work. An exciting moment.

My father took his seat high up on the machine. Reins in hand , he checked again that all was in order, put the machine in gear and our harvesting of 1935 had commenced.

Soon the farmhands commenced the job of stooking the bundles of corn which was achieved by arranging about six bundles to a stook put standing up. This procedure was followed a few days later by arranging these stooks into stacks of much larger stature and would remain so for a week or two prior to being brought to the haggard to await the annual threshing day in a month or so.

This latter was always a very major event on the farm involving about 20 people for a day or two, followed by the local grain store collecting the grain. Payment was received shortly afterwards.

My father continued cutting for a while – the corn was lively and cut and bound easily. Cow-time came however. My father took out his big watch from his waistcoat pocket and sent two farmhands home to do the milking. He and I did another round of the field but then he stopped unexpectedly. "Couldn't we do a few more rounds, the evening's so good," I said.

"No," he replied, "we are going home".

What greeted us on our return to the farmyard would imprint on both of our lives for a very long time. My mother was shouting from an upstairs window for someone to call the doctor and priest for Peg who by now was seriously ill.

The happy atmosphere of the day suddenly changed as we waited to hear what was happening upstairs.

As darkness descended on the house, my father came down and in a broken voice said: "Peg is dead".

Devastation all round.

It was a Friday. As I was going to bed I saw my parents comforting one another in the sitting-room. Night had fallen on us all.

The fine, warm, bright, hopeful morning had changed into a chilly, dark, dismal night. That fine harvest day had ended in a frightening and hopeless way.

The darkness of that day did not lift for many years afterwards.

Vincent Power is a native of Ballingarry, Co Waterford where his family has farmed since 1840. A retired bank manager, he is married with 5 children and now lives in Dublin

23 The King Of The Road

Patsy O'Brien

AFTER a lifetime looking at animal behaviour, I am left to wonder if sometimes they take on some of the characteristics of the people who owned them as they are growing up.

When I was young we got a donkey, Co Meath named Ned, from a neighbour in Knockmark, Drumree, who was a former colonel in the British Army. Obviously as an ex-officer the neighbour carried himself with a certain bearing; little did we know that his donkey prodigy would do the same.

Ned came into our small holding as a foot-soldier to help with the various labours around the farm. Before long he was running the show at animal farm level. As time went by, it got to the stage where there were times I think he was in charge of the humans as well.

Unlike many donkeys, or asses as we called them then, Ned wasn't afraid of work. But it had to be done on his terms.

For instance, as youngsters we loved to ride him out on a field and would take turns on his back. He didn't appear to mind doing it for a while but if we gilded the lily and wanted turn upon turn beyond what he considered his call of duty, he had a way of bringing our playtime to an abrupt and painful end.

I was on his back on one such occasion and he headed towards a row of thorny bushes along one side of the field. With cold-blooded calculation, he ran a line so close to the hedge that one of my legs was being swept by these brambles, necessitating a quick dismount and a painful limp back to the house to get the thorns out of my flesh.

He taught us well; after a few scrapes in such situations, we got to know when Ned had enough and didn't try to push him beyond what he was happy to do.

We also knew when to fall into line when pushing him too far on a work day. As I said, he had no fear of doing a fair shift but try to go past his point of no return and he downed tools quicker than a unionised miner in 1980s Britain.

I lost count of the number of times we would try to keep working late drawing hay or water and suddenly Ned would put a stop to our gallop. Although yoked to the cart and on the road on these occasions, he would take a unilateral decision to pull in onto the grass margin and just sit down – under the load. It was as if he had unwritten agreements in his head and if you tried to change or extend those, he rebelled.

To make matters worse, he had no mouth; they say that about a jennet or a mule but you could have pulled on the bit for ever and it made no difference to our Ned.

We grew to accept that in certain moods he wouldn't budge until the spirit moved him to get going again.

Unlike most of his species, he seemed to have an intense dislike of other animals too, particularly cows.

On one occasion my father had brought him down the road to a county council shed we used for milking our cow as it saved us having to walk her home and back every day.

As my father milked the cow he became aware that Ned was stirring outside but took little notice until the ass used his head to flick the bolt on the outside into a locked groove.

When my father had finished and tried to get out, he found himself locked in and a prisoner of Ned's whim until lunchtime. Fortunately at that stage a neighbour passing by on a bike heard the banging commotion that my father was making on the door. He then pulled back the bolt and released my father and the cow from Ned's detention.

Closer to home there was another neighbour who used the Long Acre to ensure his cow had plenty of grass. We were very fond of the owner and had no problem with this arrangement on the road close to and around our house.

However, when the unsuspecting cow extended her grazing boundaries and encroached too close to what Ned considered his territory, he jumped into action.

He headed out our gate and walked straight up to the cow in a very belligerent mood. Talk about picking a fight; he lowered his head and steamed in under the cows long neck and proceeded to drive her back whence she came. She gave him a wide berth after that.

So did my mother. One time she left a bucket of fresh milk down outside the front door and when she looked around a few seconds later, Ned was vacuuming the last few drops from the bottom of the vessel. He was an opportunist whenever the situation arose to his advantage.

Ned was 'king of our road' and was such an impressive looking brown ass; the travellers had my father pestered to see if he would sell him or swop him for one of theirs.

One day they stopped my father on the road and while talking about the possibility, the conversation was interrupted as Ned, although yoked to the car, showed amazing physical dexterity to mount the travellers' she-ass in front of the assembled multitudes.

That could in itself have led to a row except we told them

that while we wouldn't be selling or swopping Ned, they now had one of his offspring and we wouldn't charge them for that.

I can only hope that his bloodline lived on because the world was a more interesting place when Ned the Donkey was in it.

Patsy O'Brien (84) is retired farmer from Knockmark, Drumree, Co Meath and is married with five adult children and 13 grandchildren. A keen storyteller and horse racing fan, his wife is contemplating having the following inscribed on his headstone, should he go first – "Wait a minute, Mary. The last race is only starting!"

24 Last Of The Country Cures

Margaret Bourke

L IKE any student preparing to sit their Leaving Certificate, Angie was feeling nervous and unprepared as she entered the month of June. Stress levels in the household were palpable, but it was nothing Angie's mother Louise couldn't handle... or so she thought.

One evening, Louise brought a cup of tea up to Angie's bedroom where she was studying. Nothing could have prepared her for what she was about to find. Angie was lying there, wrapped up in a duvet, pale and staring into space. She noticed that Angie had a remarkably swollen jaw and looked intensely ill.

Louise was shocked to learn that there had been an outbreak of mumps in school. Angie informed her mother that the virus had spread like wildfire, and that her school had issued a health warning directed particularly toward those who were preparing for exams. Tears flowed as the potential implications of the predicament began to hit home with Louise.

This was far from an ideal scenario with the exams looming – only six days to go.

Louise knew that she needed to act... and quickly. She recalled a fascinating magazine article on the subject of ancient Irish treatments that she had recently read, but having grown up in a large town she had never actually encountered anyone blessed with a 'cure'.

Sceptical but desperate, Louise called on a friend who knew a man who practiced homeopathy – the treatment of ailments through natural means. She fixed an appointment for the following morning. That night was a difficult one as Angie's suffering seemed to be immune to any conventional medicinal relief.

The following morning, Louise was greeted by a young woman who introduced her to the man with the 'cure', Barney. He had abandoned his morning farming duties to fit Angie in. Louise was pleasantly surprised at the genuine concern displayed by these people. Something that people from the city could learn from, she thought.

Barney was once a specialist in curing mumps they learned, but was not as busy as he had once been due to the effectiveness of vaccinations.

Louise sat down alone with Barney and explained the predicament to him. He informed her that he would help them in any way that he could. He said he would seek permission from an old farmer nearby to use his premises as the cure involved walking with Angie around a working pigsty with a donkey's winkers on her head.

Louise didn't know whether he was serious or not it sounded so ridiculous. She wondered if she was mad to even consider such an outlandish remedy for her daughter.

Barney stressed that the cure depended on the host of the virus being totally aware of what was happening and while he would try and allay any fears Angie may have, Louise needed to mentally prepare her for the treatment.

The exams were now just five days away.

Louise asked Angie whether she would be prepared to undergo the 'cure' and to her surprise, she agreed immediately.

Louise called Barney and set up a meeting for later that evening where they would check out the site where the cure was to take place.

Barney drove them through winding roads to a picturesque old farm site where a very old, whitewashed stone cottage stood. An ancient looking man came to the door and led them to a grubby little pigsty. Louise was curious and itching to have a look inside the sty as she had never experienced anything quite like this before.

By this stage Barney had explained the process to Angie. He would lead her around the inside of a pigsty and through some prayers the virus would harmlessly transfer from her body to a pig's body. This transaction would take place on three consecutive days, and by the end of the third day the mumps would be cured.

Louise was instructed to return to the car. She was not comfortable with this. What mother would be? Her daughter was doing something bizarre with a stranger in an unfamiliar location.

Just as her patience ran out and she was about to get out of the car again Barney and Angie returned. As they prepared to part ways, Barney addressed only Angie. He told her to call again at the same time the next day.

Angie said she was not able to talk about what had happened if it was to work. Louise was extremely curious but knew she had to respect this. All Louise asked was that Angie was safe. She replied that of course she was and not to worry.

The next day was very similar. They went through the same routine and this time Angie seemed to have complete faith in Barney. After the second night, Angie said she felt a little better. However during the following day the swelling began in earnest in her other jaw. More pain and tears ensued.

By the final day Louise could no longer fight her curiousity and quietly followed the pair to the shed. All she could see through the darkness was Angie being led in a circle around the small dark pigsty wearing a ridiculous looking headpiece. She crept a little closer and could see that the process was finishing.

Afterwards, no money changed hands. They were simply requested to donate to a charity. On the half hour journey home, Angie began to feel better and the swelling in her face substantially reduced.

Almost simultaneously Louise began to feel unwell. They had barely pulled up outside their home when she experienced the most awful pain in her face. She ran to the bathroom but could see no swelling. Eventually she had to go to bed, terrified that she had caught the virus from her daughter.

The next day, she felt better while Angie was in great form and would have no problem sitting the exams.

Barney phoned to see how Angie was doing and Louise was delighted to report that all traces of the mumps had gone. Just before they finished their conversation, Louise told Barney what had happened in the car and how she had experienced terrible face pain.

Barney was silent for a while, then he asked whether she had left the car during the healing process. Louise admitted that she had been beside the pigsty during the conclusion of the procedure.

At that stage Barney said that he would call her back, leaving Louise perplexed and worried.

When Barney did eventually call back, Louise was

intrigued to learn why he had ended their previous phone call so abruptly. He simply said that he needed to figure a few things out.

His explanation for Louise's sudden development of symptoms was as follows: The cure takes place by the transference of the virus from the host to the nearest pig. Pigs are immune to mumps so this is generally a harmless transaction. Louise must have been closer to Angie than the pig was for the final leg of the healing process.

Barney then began to chuckle. The virus, he explained, had transferred to Louise rather than the pig, but thankfully no harm was done as the effects had already worn off. Barney jokingly informed Louise that her scepticism and curiosity could have landed her in a whole lot of trouble.

Margaret Bourke is a mother of two and a part-time office employee from Carrickmacross, Co Monaghan. She is an avid writer and prefers writing true stories. She has confirmed that the above story is true.

Cartoonist Clyde Delaney's take on Patrick O'Dwyer's story, 'The Cow That Went on Holidays', see Page 185.

... And Clyde's interpretation of Gearóid Ó Ciaráin's story, 'Fair Day In Kildysart', see Page 57.

Triplet calves on the farm of Michael Purcell.
© *Irish Farmers Journal*

Minding the cows at Bromore Cliffs. See Mike Flahive's story, 'Cows At The Cliffside', Page 77. © *Mike Flahive*

Saving the turf. See Noreen Brennan-Donoghue's story, 'A Turf Saving Deliverance', Page 31.

Opposite page and above: A potato harvest in the sixties.
See Moira Gallagher's story, 'The Potato Sowers', Page 103.
© *Irish Farmers Journal*

Picking potatoes in the 1960s. © *Irish Farmers Journal*

Breathtaking view of the majestic Minaun cliffs and an iconic picture of Martin Calvey with his famed Achill Mountain lambs, with dog Rosie standing guard. See Helen Calvey's story, 'The Day The Banshee Was Heard On Achill Island', Page 177. © *Helen Calvey*

Oats threshing in
Carnaross, Kells,
Co Meath. See James
Keane's story, 'Cuckoo
Oats and Woodcock
Hay', Page 153.
© *Irish Farmers Journal*

Pea vining in 1964. © *Irish Farmers Journal*

Taking a break from making hay in Farran, Co Cork. Picture courtesy Eileen Ludlow, see story 'The Secret Killer', Page 107.

Frank the 'Pikeman of Lough Carra' (left) and his son Al who related the story 'The White Face' in this collection, Page 85.

A scene that dominated the spring tilling across Ireland up to the 1950s and 60s as a farmer ploughs with a horse. See Mark McGaugh's story, 'The First Ploughing Day Of Spring', Page 95. © *Irish Farmers Journal*

One man and his dog drive ewes along a road to a new pasture. See Helan Calvey's story, 'The Day The Banshee Was Heard On Achill Island', Page 177. © *Irish Farmers Journal*

A man pitches as another makes a rick of hay for winter feeding.
© *Irish Farmers Journal*

Gabriel O'Gara's cow which gave birth to three calves in 1965.
© *Irish Farmers Journal*

Macra field day in Tallaght.
© *Irish Farmers Journal*

John Moran on his Galway farm. See Dan Daly's
story, 'The Threshing', Page 21. © *Irish Farmers Journal*

Cartoonist Clyde Delaney's take on Johnny
Flynn's story, 'The Maypole', Page 209.

25 Crossing The Great Divide

Declan Coyle

'**W**AS it the heart?" they asked, "or what happened to him at all?" So many people were asking how my father died and what happened on the August 3, 1987.

It was the heart. An 84-year-old heart and a recent chest infection. "And I was only talking to him a few weeks ago," they said, somewhere, someplace. He died at 12.15 in the afternoon on the Monday of the August bank holiday.

For about 10 years before he died I was living with the thought of that dreaded telephone call. The one that would say: "Come quickly, Daddy's dying." But it never came. Not in the sense that I had been expecting it. In 1977, I was in Dublin visiting my brother when the call came that Daddy had had a stroke.

When we got home he was upstairs in bed. No feeling in his right side. But he had no problem talking.

"What time are you getting up in the morning?" he asked me. (I was a Columban missionary priest at the time and I was home on holidays from Philippines.)

"About eight o'clock," I said.

"Give me a call because I'm selling 200 cattle up in Naper's at nine o'clock."

"Will you be able for it?" I asked.

"All I have to do is lane (lean) agin (against) a wall and if I can see them, I can sell them," he said matter of factly.

The following morning we headed through Oldcastle and out the Millbrook road to Naper's.

Outside the cattle pen there was a workman with blue well-worn dungarees. "Come here, gasson," Daddy shouted over to him. He came over and the pair headed for the yard. There were cattle to sell and the day was young.

My father didn't have time for a stroke at 74 years of age. Bit by bit, the feeling returned to his right side. He never looked back from that day's selling.

Except for the diabetes battle that caused many a skirmish at the table. "Daddy, you're not supposed to be eating that gooey cake."

"Well, I'll take a little bit in case you might think I'm going odd."

Then every so often it would be up to the hospital in Navan for a "kune-up." (In Cavan the "hs" all turned into "ks". A tube was a kube. Hughie was always pronounced Kughie.)

The struggle with diabetes was a constant one strewn with broken hospital visits and promises. One time in Cavan the doctor warned him: "If you don't lose over three stone within the next six months, you'll never cross 60."

"Ara, me gasson, I'm past 70 already," he purred with delight.

In his prime he tipped the scale at 22st but in the later years he dropped to a handy 18st.

Apart from the first stroke and the "kune-up" visits to the hospital, he was generally in fine fettle for his last decade. Two weeks before he died he was pitching bales of hay, and the week before he was at the cattle mart in Ballyjamesduff.

When he came home from the mart he went down to Brady's where they say he got a "turn". I got the call that he had gone into hospital the night before but that he was okay. It wasn't critical.

At that time we thought he was just in for a check-up and that he'd be out right as rain in no time. In fact he wasn't taking it too seriously himself. He got endless comfort out of the fact that the hay was baled.

In the hospital he was blessed to have a cattleman from Stradone in the next bed. "They were talking about cattle at six this morning," said the man in the other bed with the soft rolling midland accent of Offaly, "and they were talking about cattle until dinner time, and when they wheeled me down for the operation they were talking about cattle, and when I woke up tonight they were still going strong about marts, and prices, and great cattle and bad ones and one that done a terror."

While he was in hospital he got quite a few more small 'turns'. In our tribe between Loughcrew and Lough Sheelin, no one ever died of any medically known disease. Anyone who ever died in Dungimmon did it after they "got a bit of a turn".

I was with him when he got another turn.

"Call the doctor," he said, "I'm not too good."

It was one of his lowest days. Later, I went to go out to go to the toilet and he called me back and whispered: "Don't leave me! I need you here now."

So I told him that I wasn't going anywhere, to hold on and I'd be back in a jiffy. Then he relaxed again.

That got me thinking about a test they did on babies one time, and the most piercing screams came not when the babies were beaten or pinched, but when they were abandoned.

That fear of being left alone. So I made it very clear that I had no plans and that whatever happened I would be there with him.

Later that day he picked up enough to say: "Today or tomorrow will whip me, you wait and see. I have that feeling."

The pastoral care sister came to see him. They had a bit of a chat. He told her: "I want a Mass for a happy death at about seven this evening. I'll die about seven."

By eight o'clock he seemed to have forgotten about dying. "Now," I said, "what's all this crack about dying?"

"Ara, I could work yet," he said, "I'll work tonight anyway."

The following morning he was bright as a button. Shaved, hair washed and the old blue eyes sparkling – he looked like a bigger and better version of Cary Grant.

He was all business. "Ring Seán Farrelly," he instructed me. "Tell him to take 11 cattle out of Masterson's and get them into Balladuff. Hurry up or you'll be late for the killing. And Monday's a bank holiday. The prices may drop over the weekend. While you're at it run down and give Sean a hand bringing in the cattle."

"Will Seán know which eleven cattle?"

"He'll know. He'll know," he said in a loud whisper shaking his head like a man running out of patience with a simpleton.

Seán contacted the factory but they said that the killing was over for the day. They rang him back later to say they'd be out to look at the cattle first thing on Monday morning, even if it was a bank holiday. They were 93 pence, but if they were good ones they'd go 94 or 95. For really good ones they could go to 96 or 97 pence. Now whether that's an ounce, a pound, a kilo or a ton I'm not sure.

I found out later that Daddy's very good friend and cattle dealing soul mate Joe Dillon also phoned the factory and told them that an old friend of his was dying and he wanted the very best price for his 11 cattle delivered first thing on the Monday.

He told them that if they didn't give him the top price he'd never sell them another bullock for as long as he lived.

I don't think there was a day that Joe wasn't in to see him. They used to meet at all the marts and were continually visiting each other to share insights on great cattle and where the bargains were.

When to buy.

And when to sell.

That bank holiday Sunday afternoon Joe sat with him without speaking. Just nods and headshakes. The secret code of cattlemen.

His God waiting on the other side of the great divide knew the lives of the good cattlemen who gave his word and then would keep it.

The nurse warned me to not allow any visitors in except immediate family, and, of course, she says, pointing to Joe, "his brother."

The factory gave us the best prices possible and when I whispered that to Daddy early on the Monday, he smiled.

Joe Dillon knew more than we did; that a cattleman on the cusp of the great divide could die happy when he knows he's sold his bullocks at the top of the market.

Declan Coyle is the well-known author of the best-selling book, 'The Green Platform', and his new book 'Living the Green Platform' is just published. A former Columban missionary, he played football with Cavan and is married with three children.

AROUND THE FARM GATE

26 Seasons In Scenes And Sounds

Joe Keane

I DO not like change. I feel comfortable with the familiar things; like the scent of freshly mown grass on a summer day; spring lambs cavorting in a lush grassy knoll; the whitethorn and the sycamore displaying their distinctive blossoms.

As a child I stood entranced by the sound of a tenor voice wafting across the fields. The singer was John McCormack with his captivating rendering of Yeats' melody: 'Down by the Sally Garden'.

The biggest regret is the disappearance of the familiar sounds of yesteryear. The melodious whistling of the postman as he cheerfully did his daily rounds. His delightful rendering of the reel 'The Mason's Apron' resonating in the frosty morning air. In those days many people whistled with varying degrees of expertise as they went about their daily chores.

The beginning of spring saw the first outing of the ploughman. The pristine lea field would be scored with the precision of a surgical knife. As the curlews soared in ever increasing numbers on the exposed sub soil, the very heavens seemed to cry and lament. The solitary figure of the farmer against the enormity of the cumulus sky presented an awesome spectacle. Presently the unspoiled green field would be transformed into a canvas of burnt umber. In due course the tilled ground would produce the familiar green buds of the potato plant. But not before the spliced slits of the tuber were placed in orderly fashion in the fertile ridge.

The task of splicing the potato tuber requires a special skill. A local woman was employed to carry out the delicate procedure. Sheila's arrival in our house would be greeted with all the aplomb befitting a royal personage. As she worked her way through the bags of potatoes, she hummed and lilted the old tunes and ditties.

The sound of the blackbird still majestically reigns supreme amongst the creatures of the air. But the lapwings rustling flight as they take off from the nearby lake seem rarer than before. The heron is sometimes visible on a dark winters evening on the shores of the river, its presence regarded by some as an omen of bad weather. The corncrake is almost an extinct species today. His somewhat monotonous sound emanating from his secret meadow retreat was once the signal that the haymaking season was imminent.

Modern agricultural methods have proved detrimental to this foreign visitor.

One evening long ago I was playing in the evening dusk when I heard the sound of the snipe in the evening sky. The wind rustling through its wings emitted a goat-like sound. Although the bird was invisible against the darkening sky its mournful whine seemed to draw me towards it.

The cuckoo's unique sound heralded the approach of bog work. For some they approached the matter quietly cycling to the bog, the essential tools attached to the frame. In others, it brought out a pioneering zeal. One neighbour dressed in a Mexican like garment complete with sombrero. On his cart was a vast variety of cooking accoutrements. He took along an ample supply of drinking water with the same degree of urgency as if he were trekking in an Arabian desert.

The bog resembled a Red Indian reservation rather more than a west of Ireland marshland. To the casual visitor the industry of turf cutting appeared secondary to the social scene that presented itself. Pale blue wisps of smoke drifted from impromptu fires strategically placed throughout the furze cutaways. The angelus bell signalled the lunch break. A cup of tea never seemed more appetising than when brewed against that backdrop.

One afternoon a latecomer to the bog shouted out that he had noticed the local publican 'tapping' a fresh barrel of porter as he passed. This comment was both malicious and calculated. The prospect of savouring a pint of the freshly tapped beverage proved too much for the younger men. Soon the turf spreaders that my father and others had engaged to assist them were stampeding towards Donegan's pub, and the turf cutting operations were suspended at least for that evening.

I accompanied an elderly neighbour many times as he took his dog and gun out on a hunting spree. We traversed a wide area of moorland teeming with the wonders of nature. This was a place of magic and joy for me. I wondered if the poet Allingham had known such a spot when he composed his 'Airy Mountain' poem. Amongst the wild roses and blue berries, the terrain dropped in to steep valleys. Woodcock and pheasant emerged with regularity. I was secretly pleased when my adult companion bagged few or none at all, blaming the cartridges for his poor marksmanship.

On one occasion we dropped in to a mountain cottage, where an elderly man was busy making a creel. Many rural folk acquired the skill of weaving sally rods to create items of use in the home. His practiced fingers ran the rods in diverse directions and soon the turf basket began to emerge.

Sitting contentedly at the turf fire he was pleased with the world and it with him.

Thatching was another skilful expertise that prevailed at that time. The exponent of this craft was usually lithe and agile to facilitate climbing on roofs that were often fragile. He chose his materials with great care to ensure durability against harsh winters. The thatched roofs of Irish cottages were aesthetically pleasing and ecologically sustainable.

Since the legendary tales of the Gobán Saor, the stonemason has enjoyed an esteemed place in Irish society. In my youth his pending visit to a house to raise a doorway or increase the size of a window, was awaited with eager anticipation. His arrival was anticipated for weeks and news of its progress found its way to relatives in places like New York and London. The stonemason was often asked to advise his neighbours outside his station, like settling family disputes and making wills. A stonemason always had a large funeral.

I saw the traveller Johnny Riley making saucepans in a neighbour's home. His nimble fingers created the familiar utensil, with the dexterity of a conjurer. The tools of his trade, which he carried on his back in a budget, are now no more. Johnny's wealth of original folksongs has been recorded by the likes of Joan Baez and our own Christy Moore. He did not have the street savvy to capitalise on his potential fortune and died in poverty at the age of 44.

In my head the haunting sounds from my past include 'Corraig Dtonn', that mysterious sound that emanated from the lonely shore of Aughris over 40 miles from where I grew up, near the scene of the tragic drowning of six young people over half a century ago.

The phenomenon was caused by the lapping of the waves

on the precipitous rocks. On frost laden moonlight nights, do people still hear the Corraig Dtonn around Moygara and Mullaghroe and along the shore of the ancient lake, as I did all those years ago?

Joe Keane lives with his wife in Co Mayo. Since his retirement from the insurance profession he has taken up creative writing as a hobby and a number of his stories have been published.

AROUND THE FARM GATE

27 The White Cow Whinger

Denis O'Higgins

FOR as long as I could remember she had dwelt on our small farm, a placid and bony animal totally white in colour. In fact she was the only such colourful cow in our locality. To distinguish her from our other five cows, we named her 'The White Cow'.

In fact, her full name was 'The White Cow Whinger' because when approached by anyone she emitted a low whiney sound. She expected special treatment and she always achieved her wish because any attempt to speed or rush her would usually derive the opposite result.

At the time we didn't supply milk to the creamery, as there was no collection centre within reach of our farm. In summertime we milked out in the fields rather than housing or driving the cows to the farmyard. This was the rustic way of doing things. In turn each cow had to be coaxed into a corner so that the milker could hunker down and place the white enamel bucket on the ground underneath the udder and, with his knee in touch with the cow's leg, begin the milking process.

It was important to remain in knee contact to detect any sudden movement because if the cow attempted to lash-out with a kick, a rapid exit response was imperative to save the operator being sprawled on the ground with the precious milk washing over him.

When a bucket reached the full mark of the white frothy liquid it was covered with a clean cloth and placed on top of a nearby tall stonewall, while the second pale was being milked. Then both vessels were carried home by hand. Always before leaving, the traditional ritual would be fulfilled by dipping the index finger in the milky froth and make the sign of the cross on the cow's side while uttering the farming prayer of "God Bless the cow".

'The White Cow Whinger' was always out of step with the rest by producing her calf each autumn. It meant she kept the house supplied with milk during the winter period when her comrades were on production sabbatical.

Ours was an arid farm devoid of piped water, well, stream or river. The barrel-stored run-off roof water didn't last long in the dry thirsty summertime. That meant the cattle had to be walked some distance along the public road to avail of the newly drilled public pump.

The only exception to participating in that long walk was 'The White' because of her slow actions; she remained on the farm where the water was drawn to her by bucket.

On the day that I ushered her onto the roadway and headed her for the October fair in Roscommon Town, it was the first time since she arrived to us as a calf that she stepped outside our farm gate.

Carrying a reins and a bucket I directed her to begin the five-mile journey towards town. As I encouraged the cow onwards I thought of how her 14 years made her old and yet I was still young though a few years older than my charge. Despite our grá for this friendly and placid animal, we couldn't chance to keep her any longer because if she died we couldn't afford the financial loss and there was no provision for sentiment within farming.

At first our progress was slow, as my cow couldn't resist feeding on the lush sweet grass growing on the long acre. Now and then she would dip her head into one of the many deep potholes in the rough stony surface and vacuum out a huge drink.

When she had eaten and drunk her fill, I coaxed her into a faster stride and luckily at the turn I met up with a neighbouring farmer who was setting out with his four steers. We decided that two herds were better than one and joined forces. This made it easier to block off the many gaps; open gateways and side roads while the companion eased the cattle past the plethora of natural obstacles and barking dogs as we drove onwards.

By the time we reached the town it was almost bright. By then, many other farmers had arrived before us and taken up the prime display areas to accommodate and show their livestock. Using one end of my reins I made a halter, placed it around the cow's head and tied the other end to the railings of that large empty building in the Town Square known as The Harrison Hall. I utilised the bucket to milk her and afterwards used the pail to keep her well watered.

I waited and waited hoping that some dealer would take an interest in my bony old cow. While she did get the odd visual inspection and questions were asked about her age and milk production, I did not get any concrete offers.

In the afternoon an elderly gentleman approached me. He was so well dressed that his attire made him appear out of place as a jobber. Along with his black suit and tie he wore a pocket-watch and a neat hat and sported a handlebar moustache. I answered all his questions except by fibbing that "I wasn't sure" when he asked me about her age. To satisfy the age requirement this small man attempted the normal practice of teeth inspection.

When he attempted to open the cow's mouth, she objected by jerking her head upwards and almost knocking him down in the process. He left the age question unanswered. He then offered me £16 to purchase her, but I had been advised before leaving home not to take less than £20.

I insisted on a price of £24. I knew I was on shaky ground as his was the only bid I had all morning, but £19-10-0 was his final offer before he began to walk away.

When I decided to accept, he returned, and taking out a small tin-box, he drew a red mark across her white head while insisting: "I'll have to get some luck out of that." I promised him that I would treat him right. He advised me to stay in charge of the animal until he returned later with the cash payment. In the meantime other potential dealers glanced at my cow but when the red mark was noticed they looked no further as that was the universal "Sold sign" indication.

While enduring the long wait, and hoping that the buyer would keep his word by returning, I was kept amused with the antics of the Cheap-Jack who had pitched his wares nearby. As always, in order to commandeer the best stand he was the earliest arrival at the fair. He spread his items of delph and aluminium goods on the hard surface. He used many ruses to attract the crowd and then humoured them into finding a need to purchase one or more of his household products, which he sold for a few pence less than charged in the shops.

I recall watching an elderly man lift a chamber pot and ask in a timid voice "what price is this" when the Cheap-Jack pretended not to hear and ignored him, the potential customer repeated his question in a louder voice and only then, when the bystanders began to listen and take heed, did the Cheap-Jack acknowledge him by replying "if you can fill it you can take it with you for nothing".

Eventually my buyer returned and I helped him chaperone the cow down Castle Street where he closed her into a small meadow beyond the crossroads. He then took a wad of pound notes from his breast pocket and counted out nineteen to me, while he retained the last ten shillings as his "luck penny".

I was concerned as it was normal for the seller to decide, and the sum he retained was well above the going rate. I had intended returning five shillings to him but now this wasn't to be. However I parted company with the dealer and had a last long look at 'The White Cow Whinger' as she tried to come to terms with the strange surroundings.

Walking homeward out the Athlone Road, I had reached Molly's hill before any traffic passed. It was a small pick-up truck and the driver, our local postman, who was also a part-time jobber, gave me a lift to the crossroads.

I walked home the last half mile and as I drew level with our farm the realisation dawned, that the White Cow Whinger was no longer part of our herd. It made me sad that this was how it had ended.

I checked my pocket once more, touched the bundle of notes and headed in the door with a heavy heart.

Denis O'Higgins is a native of Knockcroghery, Co Roscommon and is a former wildlife ranger for the Department of the Environment. Married with a daughter, his hobbies include walking, reading, travel, history and writing.

28 Taming Sally

Jim McNamara

THE grey revolver came in a padded metallic case. "Are you sure you want to be here for this?" the vet Garry asked.

It won't be easy on you, but trust me it's much easier on her, she's a big animal and she'll need a lot of injections which would take a long time."

I want to be with her. She's been there for me for nearly 20 years. It was the least I could do.

It was a loud quick blow, close to the centre of the skull. The head fell flat on its side, followed by two stretching kicks of the hind legs and a little trickle of blood from the nose. "She's out of her pain," he said reassuringly.

Sally had begun her life in fields near Kilrush, close to a road along the Wild Atlantic Way. Her wider family of seven others included three mares, two sister foals and two yearlings that ran as a group over sand dunes, low fences, and small roads.

They sheltered in Dan's shed only in the cold of winter, where they fed on round bales of hay after the fields grew bare. Dan's was a two storey farmhouse with a low-walled front lawn that was always bare. No lawn mower was ever needed as the horses regularly pushed open the small gate for the sheltered new grass as soon as it appeared.

Dan appeared at his front door and greeted the visitors

with a few crusts of bread. Sally and her sisters quickly scurried out the small gate, but the elders accepted the kindness.

That autumn in the feeding shed Dan tightened the space with a flexible gate. He introduced a home-made rope head collar that wrapped around the top of the head behind the ears and came down close to the mouth at each side, making two knots and leaving a few inches hanging down. He placed a double bag of hay over each foal's back. This was almost empty at the top and hung down at the sides, an extra intrusion, but with little room to run and shake it off was just about tolerated.

The mares were bareback ridden regularly with the foals running by the side. Sally could now be caught by the head collar occasionally as she trotted close by. Soon her hay bags hanging in the shed were swapped for Dan himself. She protested, but Dan could easily move from mother to daughter and back again in the tight space of the covered shed.

When the time came for Sally to be sold and exit the West Coast of Clare the advertisement was put in *Buy And Sell*. 'Connemara Mare, well-trained, ideal for children. Price €1200.'

A deal was quickly reached for the now excellently trained mare with a new family, and Dan agreed to personally deliver her as part of the package.

Later that week, Sally arrived in a single wooden box pulled by a white Volvo 740. "Keep her in the smallest patch possible or she'll fatten. She'll give you several foals too," Dan said, with a final pat to her neck.

The morning brought out the excited new owners. Mick had his own bridle made of proper leather for Sally. He could ride bare back ok but the children could ride only on saddled horses.

The brown hard leather structure was designed for a smaller pony. Sally at fifteen hands was not pleased. The back pads pinched. Two iron foot stirrups hung half way down either side and the tightened bellystrap was irritating.

Mike uncomfortably positioned himself on the saddle struggling to get his feet into the stirrups. She tolerated the unwieldy structure and they managed a trot into another field and back without major drama. Next the children. Ten year old Tom needed a leg up and with a lead from his father; all three managed a circle of the smaller field. "Me now, me now," his sister Marion called and when her turn came another circle of the same field was led by Mike. A bond was forming.

That winter Sally and Mike drew out small trees together from the woods. Over the ditch were two leggy half-bred hunters with padded blanket covers looking on, with what seemed a curious grin. They were show horses, trained, groomed and stable fed for the "Cheers all" of the local hunt.

Further down the road was a group of mixed horses and a strong grey stallion. When the season came Sally spent a week there and a tiny spindle-legged foal was the outcome. Two more foals were to follow and despite the best efforts of local trainers only one of the three was prepared to yield to carrot, cuddles or whip.

The mornings were Sally's best times, just at dawn with fresh dew, she would wrap both lips around the tufts of grass held between her teeth and suck in rhythm with the cutting and pulling. After an hour or two, fully content she would lie down, near her small foal, joined by a few hopping small birds.

Her own family circle, though diminished since leaving Dan, was beginning to restore itself. Here was a little foal nestling in beside her, part of her own flesh and bone. He was now three months old, full of joy and mischief.

As she and her foal fell into a misty sleep, her dream was of wide open space and of being free, of a great harmony between humans and all creatures of the wild, without the use of whips or cages. She had something of a free spirit in the way her eye watched attentively to what was going on.

Sally had two more foals and continued to work the wood, as well as giving the occasional ride to visiting children, but she became slower to move and began to put on more weight. Her feet had started to give her trouble. Her carers confined her to a smaller paddock, but her feet still hurt badly. A local vet who cared for the sheep was called when her limping became more painful.

"An infection" he stated, putting her on a course of antibiotics and a worm dose. After short-lived relief she began to struggle again. Her walk became a kind of horse crawl and she had major trouble standing up. A specialist horse vet was called this time and immediately identified "advanced laminitis", a disease of domesticated horses. There was now only one option.

When the truck arrived, a long hoist was extended over its sides. Sally's cover was removed and a small chain was wrapped around her front and back legs, which were now folded together. Gently the driver lifted her and turned the remains to lower her into the back. She lay lifeless beside an older cow and two small lambs at the front. The lorry's contents were covered tightly. The driver was paid and left.

That night the family visited the spot where she laid and

collected the blood stained cover. "Her DNA is still with us" said Thomas.

All was quiet now, but for a distant bark of a dog near the village. A tiny moon was rising in the east. Looking south a group of four stars formed a square over the wood, with two small extra ones at the top corner."

"Aren't they kind of like her ears?" said Marion. And they really were.

Jim McNamara is an organic farmer and founder An tIonad Glas- the Organic College in Dromcollogher Co Limerick. Married with three children, he is co-author of the herb book Cluain Chumhra; Fragrant Meadow.

29 Cuckoo Oats And Woodcock Hay

James Keane

NYONE familiar with Macamore land will know that the soil is heavy and marly and that when it gets wet it turns to muck, and when it gets too dry it cracks. That never stopped, however, some farmers from sowing an odd field of spring barely or oats.

The margins would always be very tight, of course, and then you would have to hope to get a favourable year; sure you might only gain the few bales of straw.

Either way, it was good sometimes to plough the land, sow it down or reseed it, especially if you wanted to level it and straighten out any visible furrows from the one sod.

The back field in Bats was our best field and it had not been ploughed since the forties when the Compulsory Tillage Order was in place; department officials at that time had apparently visited the crop and marvelled at its robust growth. My grandfather was the boss then, so it was a big event to be ploughing it now about 60 years later.

The silvery boards of the plough shimmered and barely seemed able to keep pace with the soil as it rushed to be turned over. Within half an hour, it had surpassed what a good man and a horse could have done in one good day.

Punching above its weight again, the back field yielded a crop worthy of comparison with those in the dry land; the cast of barley was as thick as a forest and the grain was full and round; that last few months of good sun really crowned it. So when the autumn delivered the blue skies, and the sun shining so high, it was perfect for baling and impossible to go to school for that one day.

I divided my time on the tractor with my father as we re-windrowed the straw before the baler got to work.

At other times I ran between the lines of straw, which constantly structured my career of play, and counted the bales in each row, and then reported back to say there will be at least another 15 bales and that it was likely to work out at 10 bales to the acre after all. In the background, the baler kept on clunking and gleaning and stopping to roll another majestic golden bale to which I would run and climb.

From a bale, I was the one who first noticed the snout of the car entering the field and making its way along the headland towards the watery marl hole.

With no threat of rain and rush for the baler to be anywhere else that evening, the men appeared to get off their respective tractor in mid-sentence. In moments like this, I knew not to talk.

With his back to the front wheel, Jimmy settled into the tea and sandwiches that my mother deftly arranged without a disruption to the flow of talk between the two men. Whenever plates were emptying, she would top them up from the carrier bag or if the ham sandwiches were getting low she would take one from me and place it on Jimmy's plate and then my father would give one of his away before everything would settle back and they would slash the last sup of tea from the cup onto the ground before another re-fill. I drank my tea fast so I could mimic the men and slash it out and get another cup.

"You could live in that weather," said Jimmy.

"You surely could," said my father. "Cuckoo oats and woodcock hay will make the farmer run away; sure haven't we had a great time this year, it's a joy to do anything".

"I'd say the young man doesn't know what you mean by that?" Asked Jimmy.

I shook my head.

"Well," Jimmy explained, "if the spring is so backward that the crops can't be sown until the cuckoo is heard around April and the hay can't be got until the woodcock shoots in November then the farmer will be gone beside himself with worry. It's the both together in one year that's the killer, eh?

"Yeah", said my father. "You might get away with cuckoo oats around here but it wouldn't be good. I often remember dragging in late hay from the ricks and the wall against the feeder would be black and crawling with the slugs from the hay. I don't know how cattle survived on it. Sure there was little to make anything with in those days and the labour involved... some cocking on a hundred ricks... wasn't the modern baler a great thing?"

"They were surely better than the old ones," said Jimmy.

A slash of tea fired across my feet.

"Would you look at the water hens," continued Jimmy, "haven't they great cover on that marl hole... most innocent little bird of them all".

"The drainage scheme was a great thing for this part of the country."

"Haughey brought that in in the 60s, didn't he?" quizzed Jimmy.

"He did indeed," answered me father.

The sun baked heat into every crevice and my body

hummed with contentment as I sat there hanging off every word.

"Do you know what I haven't seen in years", said Jimmy, "the gadfly. The gadfly was a terror for attackin the cattle. Sure you'd know all about it around here."

"The gadfly," replied my father, "was more or less done away with when all the scrub and cover on the fields were levelled out when they were doing the drainage. The sprays and the different things on the crops these days would have hindered them too. Sure that time there was no such thing as a firm gap or fence; there were two or three fields to every one field now. The cattle had great cover but it was a nightmare trying to find a missing beast, especially if the gadfly was about."

"Yes, I remember up near me we would run to tell the local farmer if the cows were gadding," interjected my mother.

The day was going on and it was time to end the chatting.

Jimmy rose and squinted towards the retiring sun and said, "You know, I hates the sight of the sun setting on a day like this. I won't be long knocking the rest of this out of it. Missus, thank you for the tea."

Jimmy turned to me and asked: "You wanna join me for the last few bales young man? It'll keep you out of reach from the gadfly should he appear."

With that, Jimmy threw his head back and laughed, took a few sprightly steps, began revving and giddying the baler to clunk dust into orbit again, turn her to the sun, until we were off away, with me as co-pilot.

My mind bobbed with delight wondering about the gadfly and the bales I had yet to climb and the water hens I was going to count but as we turned her for the sun each time, I only wished that those last few windrows were a little longer, and the evening too, just a little longer.

James Keane is a teacher from Ballygarrett, Co. Wexford. He now spends most of his time living and working on the family farm with his father Seamus.

AROUND THE FARM GATE

30 Maps, Gaps And Patchwork Fields

Catherine Power Evans

THE topography of my childhood home was a lazy sprawl of patchwork fields. Throughout the year the pastureland displayed a tapestry of colours: greens, yellows and browns, over a range of embroidered textures as they were worked or grazed.

Along the narrow road on which we lived were familiar farm gates upon which our little grazed legs climbed, simply because they invited us.

The countryside was ours to roam freely. No one stopped us traipsing through farmland in our search for amusement in the streams and rivers between gentle valleys criss-crossing the landscape.

Our outdoor ceiling was a great big sky, spread across rural Waterford in a world that no longer exists as it did. Life and childhood followed the cadence of the seasons and elements, and we felt nature move.

As winter gave way to a new, verdant spring, our bodies took on the vigour of newborn lambs, calves and foals that frolicked in dewdrop fields. Our limbs lengthened and we could jump higher, run faster, and for longer. Knowledge of how the world – our world – worked built up through physical and cognitive interaction, assimilating the cosy microcosm of the homeland into internal maps.

Just as the streets in the small town had names, so too did

our local fields. The Soccer Field played host, briefly, to the local soccer team; the Bog Field was designated for grazing due to poor drainage; the Forty-Acre Field – well, that's self-explanatory. Now, fields named after their owners have changed identity after the demise of old farmers. The gate of one such field lay across the road from my home and was the starting point of many an adventure, when a cascade of sun-browned legs flew over the bars in our haste for fun.

By the brow of the hill that faced the heather-covered Comeragh mountains, lay a paradox. 'Johnny McGorey's Quarry' wasn't so much that as a miniature crater, a depression on an otherwise even field. It served as a graveyard for an old Ford whose inert black bodywork provided the canvas for rust to paint permanent abstract art. Johnny was – is – a mystery, about whom a saying was told: "I'll tell you a story about Johnny McGorey. Will I begin it? That's all is in it." Its origins and purpose remain unexplained.

Each year we reacquainted ourselves with that place. We employed new tactics to breach the brutal covering of briars that had shot up with rude vigour, thwarting our ambition to sit on the mildewed, leather seats. We longed to grab the big old steering wheel and grind the gears of that once-handsome jalopy.

'Ditches' were plundered in summertime, (when the sun used to shine for longer than a mad minute). Blackberries ripened in fecund fruitfulness and we sold our fermenting pickings to the Blackberry Man. The excitement was mighty as we presented our tubs and canisters for the weekly weigh-in. Unaccustomed to wealth, the few pounds in our little purple-stained hands made us feel like millionaires.

Our quest for exploration took us miles beyond the boundaries of our house. This self-led education enabled us to learn how to avoid trouble; we checked for bulls in herds of cows before walking among them and kept alert for trains when we walked on the railway.

Wellingtons were the preferred footwear, but in summer they were abandoned for canvas runners. While these drastically reduced the stink of sweaty feet, it opened up a new hazard: after a miscalculated step landed a foot in a crusty-topped dung pancake, smelly mush would ooze over the tops of the white shoes. Feet could be washed but we feared facing Mam when we got home. The job of cleaning and re-whitening the fabric to adequately cover green stains was a 'job and a half' and we often endured a 'bother in the ear'.

The smell of cow-dung is but one of the odours of the countryside that were part and parcel of the visceral nature of the surroundings in which we were immersed. Some of the myriad smells I can recall vividly include the earthy smell of desiccated furze bushes collected for firewood; wet ground after a rain shower; the inexplicable aroma of pink-gilled mushrooms strung on stalks for carrying home; the smell of fresh hay; warm milk in the milking parlour; the scent of new calves. Then there was the musty smell of August blackberries; bacon and cabbage boiling on the range; rotting spuds in sacks in a dark outhouse and then later, the marvellous spritz released from a new season, ruddy Kerr's under the scraping thumb of a gardener inspecting the quality; and occasionally, the fetid, maggoty stench of hanging fowl and rabbits.

My family kept small numbers of animals over the years. There's a photo taken of me beside a vaguely remembered out-building that housed snorting pigs and their squealing, greedy banbhs. Cattle were fattened, destined for the long-gone Clover Meats factory. Hens provided eggs , and some even made it to the table, while turkeys were raised annually for the Christmas dinner.

A new vocabulary – that included 'lights', 'crop', 'gizzard' – was learnt when I watched, in gruesome fascination, my grandmother undertaking the task of dismembering the fowl. Stubborn feathers that evaded plucking had to be burnt off, and the smell was horrible. Smaller, downy feathers floated in the air, tickling my nose.

Pulling into the busy railway station in the little town, the train was well-used by the locals. Shop goods were delivered to the train station and collected by bicycle or van, to replenish shelves. As well as human passengers, it was common to see livestock onboard. A bus service was a boon too; my grandmother's consignment of day-old chicks were despatched by bus, then delivered and left for collection at one of the shops. A cardboard box would arrive home chirping incessantly, and when opened, a wave of yellow fluff on legs spilled out. These chicks were adorable, but soon grew into straggly, gangly pullets – if they hadn't already expired from the journey, or at the hands of a toddler who might love one to death in an over-eager chokehold.

Collecting eggs as a small child was a favourite chore; it felt magical, like I was getting presents. The hens laid in pre-ordained nests, though one might go feral. We became good scouts. Sometimes I got pecked while battling a contrary hen, vociferously protesting the removal of her fresh, warm egg. It was worth the risk when one of those wholesome, brown, speckled eggs were boiled and put in front of me for my tea, accompanied by toast, the fast food of the day.

There was an absence of ready meals in my mother's kitchen. She made dinners from scratch with stock cupboard ingredients, and the produce from the garden when in season. Life was relatively free from the clutter of gadgetry. Turning the big box of a telly off meant getting up off the chair to press a button. Changing channels presented no bother: there was only the one national station!

The only net we knew was the one over my mother's curlers, and downloading and uploading was what happened to bales on a trailer. I was acquainted with the earliest version of e-books – the contents of the alphabetically arranged E shelf in the library run by the publican's wife in their house. With the aid of a torch, I furtively devoured textual matter under the blankets.

There were no mobile phones to give directions when you got lost, or to alert family and friends when you might be late. You learned strategies to deal with situations so we could stand on our own two feet. "You'll never be lost while you have a tongue in your head," was good advice. Rural life had its hardships but its rewards were many, and the age of (relative) innocence was priceless since it cannot be recaptured.

Catherine Power Evans is a native of Kilmacthomas, Co. Waterford but now lives in West Wales with her husband and has two grown sons. She belongs to an online writing group and a number of her stories have been published.

31 The Bogeyman In The Barn

Mary Conliffe

MY father was hospitalised during the 1960s when I was about 11-years-old. It meant that I had to accompany my mother every day after school to the farm at Doon a mile away from our home at Derrinsallagh, Borris-in-Ossory to milk the cows.

Wintertime was the big challenge. In the darkness of those long dreary evenings it was hard to make out our direction on the road except for the small light of my mother's flash lamp.

We picked our way carefully to the barn close to the haggard barely able to make out where the cows stood. We heard Maisy and Daisy chewing the cud and I found this reassuring. My mother sat on a wooden stool while I sat on top of an upside down bucket beside her.

The flash lamp lit up the place and my mother directed me to use the flash lamp at the udders of the cows so that she could complete her task.

She was a brave strong woman and as I was the eldest of the family I was chosen to accompany her while my 10-year-old sister Teresa remained at home with baby Monica.

One evening while she was milking I heard a shuffling noise above us in the loft of the barn and became frightened.

"What's that strange noise?" I asked.

She pointed her flash lamp up to the loft and she just answered calmly: "The bogeyman who comes for shelter on cold winter nights. His name is Johnny and he is completely harmless and only wants a night's sleep."

I was still nervous. She continued her work with the trickling sound of the milk dropping down into the silver bucket. I wondered why she didn't want to discuss the noise in the barn loft, which had aroused my curiosity.

During busy times on the farm our father and uncles got help from local men in the area. We had to feed the men during this busy time with a hearty warm dinner when they all came back to the house. I knew them by their first names but one man had a funny nickname, Stony. He was quiet and seldom talked at the table but loved to read the Farmers Journal newspaper or the 'The Sacred Heart Messenger' magazine, copies of which were scattered around our home. He worked silently and swiftly on the farm always keeping to himself.

"Where do you come from?" I asked him.

"The great outdoors" he answered.

My sister Teresa remarked: "You sleep under the sky with all the dotted stars above you, do you never get freezing cold?"

"Yes, at times but I am closer to God in that way," was his smiling response.

"What if it rains?" we asked.

"Oh! The Good Lord will provide for me."

All the men left for their homes in the late evening after a hard day's work and we assumed, as innocent children, that Stoney would have returned to his own house.

Then on another occasion when we were milking the rustling in the loft attracted my attention again.

"Mammy, I hear the noise. Is it a ghost?" I asked, sweating and now more frightened than before.

"When we finish milking I will tell you a secret on the way home," she promised.

As we both carried the cans of milk back with us to Derrinsallagh under a star-studded sky with frost glistening like spiders' webs on the ditches, she told me the story of Stoney.

"He is a former monk from the nearby Cistercian Abbey in Roscrea who was unsuitable for communal life. His health was not strong enough for the rigorous monastic regime and so he went from farm to farm and lived like a wandering labourer.

"Perhaps that is why he was called Stoney as a rolling stone gathers no moss," she explained.

My father had employed him for odd jobs on the farm for several years because Stoney knew a lot, having worked on the monastery farm. He was accustomed to a life of silence and that explained why he did not talk as much as the other men and had no interest in that small-time gossip in which the locals engaged.

"Is he the man we hear rustling in the barn loft when we are milking the cows?" I asked.

"Yes indeed he is," my mother confirmed. She informed me that he was a beautiful singer but his only song was 'Salve Regina,' the evening hymn of the monks.

Some time after I went to work as an air hostess in Aer Lingus in 1972, I received a letter from my mother to say Johnny had passed away in hospital in Portlaoise and was now united with his heavenly stars.

Fr Purcell mentioned him at Sunday Mass in Borris-in-Ossory likening him to the famous French monk Benedict Joseph Labre, a travelling holy man in the 18th century, who was not suitable for communal life in a religious order and was known to talk rarely and pray frequently.

We were blessed to know such a spiritual and gentle

person who shunned materialism and whose philosophy of life was determined by the motto: 'God will provide.'

Mary Conliffe comes from a farming background at Doon, Borris-in-Ossory, Co. Laois. Married with two children and one grandchild, she now lives in Robertstown, Co Kildare.

32 The Best Wheat In The Barrow Valley

Tom Byrne

IT was late October in the early sixties when a letter arrived for my father saying that he was in a competition to find the best wheat grower in the catchment area which covered a good slice of the Barrow valley in counties Kildare, Laois, Carlow and Kilkenny.

We all said it must be a mistake as these prizes were always won by big farmers from around Athy, Maganey and the better wheat growing land of that region of Kildare. Our wheat was grown down on our small farm in county Carlow, which to give it its due was not bad land either.

However it turned out that it was no mistake as the manager of the co-operative sent out a message asking my father to attend a local hotel the following week where the winners would be announced.

Despite being very sceptical of getting any prize, my father dressed up in his best suit, tie and hat and headed off to Carlow. My mother and sister and I went with him in the old Ford Anglia.

There was a big crowd of farmers in for the occasion but no one from our area and my father felt a bit out of place. However the banter was good and with some food and drinks laid on, he became more at ease as time went on.

There was great talk about the harvest and the price of cattle and, of course, the weather. The tension rose as the manager called for silence and said that the results were about to be announced.

He started with the third prize and then the runner-up but there was no mention of my father and to be honest I think he was relieved not to be in the limelight.

After another call for silence and to everyone's surprise my father's name was called out for having turned out the best bushel weight of wheat supplied to the co-operative that year.

The co-op manager called him to the stage and the chairman presented him with the cup. All the other farmers gathered round, shook his hand and congratulated him on his win.

While my father was a humble and shy man I think he took great pleasure in getting one up on some of those big-shot farmers who might not have considered him in their league when it came to growing wheat.

The manager filled the cup and invited my father to take the first drink and then passed it around. There was lemonade and biscuits for all the children – a rare treat in those days.

My father was not a habitual drinker but could handle a few whiskeys if the occasion arose and this surely was one of those occasions. After a bit of celebration we were despatched with my father staying behind to do some "shopping."

As the evening wore on we waited patiently for him to arrive home. Late on a car pulled up outside and the co-op manager came in looking very sheepish, followed by my father loudly singing 'The Moon Behind the Hill' which was one of his favourite songs.

The poor manager was mortified as he thought that my mother would blame him for giving my father too much drink but he needn't have worried as my mother knew that he would sleep it off and be alright in the morning.

Although none of the rest of us slept very well that night we were still up with all the excitement early next morning. My father was already up and gone for the cows to do the milking. When he came in for his mid-morning tea my mother gave him a bit of a ribbing about drinking to excess but it was all in good spirit.

There was also a bit of talk about the cup. It stood on the dresser in the kitchen for a long time afterwards and was always the subject of conversation when neighbours called in or if we had visitors.

When the local paper came out the following week there was an article on our win in the wheat competition under a headline: 'Carlow man grows the best wheat.'

Prompted by this publicity, that evening all the neighbours and local small farmers came to our house to congratulate my father on his win. My mother put out the best table cloth and china and made tea and sandwiches for all as if it was a threshing. As the evening wore on there was also a few bottles of stout and the odd whiskey drank to salute his achievement.

Amongst the men there was a great sense that this was a victory for the small farmer against the big one and you could see they took great pride and satisfaction that on this occasion, it was one of their own who had come out on top.

Tom Byrne hails from Garryhill, Co Carlow and runs the family engineering business as well as farming part-time. Married with grown up children, he is interested in local history and writing.

33 The Quiet Man

Eileen Casey

IT'S not every day 'The Duke' steps into an Irish kitchen but that's what happened to my brother-in-law. In true rural storytelling tradition, Gerry can tell a tale from his childhood that can hold its own in any company.

Born and bred on a small farm in Milehill, Ballinrobe, County Mayo, he knows that such a good story, like the finest salmon, needs a strong 'hook' to reel it in.

Cast your mind back to the early 1950s when John Wayne, a giant in stature and a giant among Hollywood stars was filming 'The Quiet Man' in Cong, County Mayo. Directed by John Forde, the film co-starred our own beautiful Maureen O'Hara. Gerry was 10-years-old at the time and a valuable pair of hands on the family farm.

Gerry had no sisters but his flock of older brothers helped out also with the chores. His mother was industrious, rearing free range chickens for the table and for the sale of their eggs. Together with the eggs she also sold country butter and cream to Ashford Castle at Cong, where John Wayne (real name Marion Mitchell Morrison) hung his hat for the duration of filming *The Quiet Man*.

When telling this tale, Gerry often pauses to savour the fact that playing cowboys and 'injins' was every young boy's favourite game back then. Any time spared from schoolwork or chores around the farm was spent scouting out warrior braves. This entailed wriggling through daisy and buttercup flecked fields with an imaginary rifle (the more enterprising used sticks 'lanced' with a piece of twine) or creating ambush sites behind stooks of hay or water barrels. Dried (or still moist) cowpats had to be avoided in the fields while around the yard, going under the radar of the homestead's barking collie provided the challenge. Wayne's film *Red River* (released in the late 1940s) about a cattleman driving his herd north on the Chisholm Trail resulted in Gerry's renewed interest in the small dairy cattle herd on the Grimes' farm. Well, a boy could dream couldn't he? So, the magical excitement stirred up by the arrival of Hollywood's leading man into his own kitchen can hardly be imagined.

It was mid-morning, a Saturday and no school. The glass jars which held the linen coloured cream were scalded and dried and filled with their prized contents, neatly stacked in a cardboard box in the small refrigerator that hummed and shuddered in the corner of the kitchen. Gerry's father and his brothers were out working in one of the back fields.

Gerry watched his mother bustle about, placing the fragile eggs with luminous tinted shells into trays, both mother and son listening for the car from Ashford which came once every fortnight to collect the standing order.

Gerry's thoughts wondered to the sleek black car meandering along the road from Cong to Milehill. By the time it swung into the concrete yard, his head was full with fanciful notions. Then two men stood in the doorway, one was Michael, the driver of the car from Ashford and well known to them over the years. The other, towering over him, had to stoop under the lintel as he entered – it was none other than John Wayne.

"I've brought a visitor," Michael said, introducing his famous companion and winking at mother and son. Gerry's mother reached out her hand in welcome. Gerry stepped forward as he was introduced and, under the gaze of those sea-blue eyes, suddenly felt awkward, like a young colt's first straightening on his long legs.

Tea was offered to Mr Wayne and accepted (made from real tea leaves). Gerry watched him drink it, half expecting him to throw the last drops down on the floor as he'd seen him do many a time when dousing a campfire.

The fruit tart cooling on a tray near the Stanley range was refused though 'The Duke' did say that it looked "mighty fine". He complimented the well-kept garden patch near the door where pots of geranium and silky begonias shone with light and summer brightness.

The star also asked about the chickens that scattered in every direction as the car entered the yard. He was interested in their feeding rituals and the woman of the house explained the merits of dry grains mixed with green foods such as cabbage and how to spot a healthy bird.

John Wayne's voice was deep and rich and it filled the kitchen with a low musical drawl that had not been heard there before. There was a gentleness about him despite his size that was noted and remarked upon each time the tale was told.

Gerry still hadn't found his tongue when the time had come to load up the car with the boxes from the fridge (a task that John Wayne was only too eager to help with) and take leave of their visitors.

A silver dollar was pressed into his hand by the brightest silver screen star of that time – that dollar is still in his possession to this day.

When Gerry's father and brothers returned that day, they didn't seem to be bothered that they had missed such an unexpected occurrence.

However, as time went by, they felt they missed out on a great moment of popular culture. They didn't have the silver dollar like Gerry had, but they decided to name one of the lower fields 'The John Wayne' so that the historic visit would live on everytime the field was mentioned.

Eileen Casey is originally from the Midlands but currently lives in South Dublin. Her poetry and prose has been widely published. She works as a creative writing tutor.

34 The Day The Banshee Was Heard On Achill Island

Helen Calvey

IF only all farms were equal and blessed with the boundary of a farm gate. Not so in this wild and rugged Island of Achill where the vast commonages of the estate of the Rev. Edward Nangle remain. As a young girl back in the late 80s it was exactly these open free range commonages that kept me awake at night.

We farmed Mayo Blackface Sheep and every May as sure as the cuckoo would grace us with her presence and start to sing, we the Calvey Family were called for the "tagging". There was nothing that could make my heart sink faster than the knowledge that the mighty Sliabh Mór was calling and the hundreds of wild blackface sheep were to be gathered. Not least that the sheep grazed the whole mountain but the fact that there were no fences or gates meant the sheep were well and truly wild.

Hailing from a large family of two boys and eight girls, the task of the gathering was made less daunting. On previous expeditions I had been graded as a lowland gatherer and rarely was asked to scale the peaks of Creag na Mban and the Star that stood proud like beacons out of the crevices of the 2,200ft mountain.

However, on this particular May afternoon, five of us left for the mountain; my two siblings, Sarah and Orla, my father and our right hand man Ray. I was dispatched to the old Marconi Tower to collect two ewes. The Marconi tower stood atop of the adjacent hill. My father Martin had spotted the ewes with his spying glass. I was delighted to have been given first-hand instructions as the difficulty of having no mobile phones back then meant that one had to be fluent in hand gesturing.

With this prized information I journeyed off, carefully zig-zagging the hill as my father had taught me too. Orla and Sarah were dispatched to the lofty heights of Sliabh Mór and Ray was sent to the back of the mountain called Dirk.

Out on the hills and valleys I was alone and I could sing to my heart's content. We usually entered the Mayo Fleadh Cheoil each May and I would practise the Sean Nos songs as I ascended the hill. My multitasking abilities were clear at the tender age of 10.

On arrival at my destination there was no sign of the ewes – only the bold Atlantic Ocean and the view stretched up the entire coastline of North Mayo. Momentarily I took in my surroundings looking west to Croughan Mountain home of the tallest Sea Cliffs in Europe. I almost forgot the task that lay before me. It was a scene of absolute and perfect beauty.

Just then I heard a lazy bleat behind me and there I spied my quarry. Part of me couldn't believe how easy this task was, there were my two ewes and all I had to do was get them down the mountain and into the collection point at the Deserted Village that stood lonely and bleak at the front of Silabh Mór.

I made a noise – something like "sheeeeth" – which startled the sheep; they took off at pace. I ran as fast as I could after them down the hill. The ewes were travelling much quicker than I could but I caught sight at one point of my two sisters with their freshly gathered flock. They were descending Sliabh Mór and I was descending "The Tower" straight into the valley floor between them.

As my sheep were running in their direction I slowed, thinking the animals would join the others. Instead they just kept running and when the larger flock saw them they started running too. They weren't going in the direction we wanted but were gathering pace in the direction of the bottom of the Valley and out around the back to Dirk and the Coves.

Not even Usain Bolt would have caught them. I could tell by the expressions on my sisters' faces that all was not well. My sister, Orla, told me that it was all my fault the sheep had escaped and were by now miles out the back of the mountain or lost in the cove.

I could feel the hot tears about to flow when Sarah, our eight-year-old sister, said she had enough of her two sisters and just started bawling. I joined in and Orla – realising the futility of the situation – joined us.

What were we like? Three young girls on the side of a remote mountain bawling and wailing like banshees.

We knew what lay ahead somewhere in front of us was Dad no doubt waiting for us to come down the mountain with the sheep. We weren't for moving and to this day I do not know how long we sat there, but we just kept wailing.

Dad arrived on the scene and rather than the usual jump to attention we were so deflated we just sat there. The expression on his face was unreadable. He appeared genuinely concerned as to what was going on, telling us he thought we were banshees.

When he asked us what on earth was so terrible that we were in such a state, between our sobs and wailing, he grasped that the sheep were gone.

Just as we were about to stand up and face the reality of hours of hard work gone down the drain, the sheep miraculously appeared behind us, ascending out of the Valley. Out of thin air came those wild Achill Sheep with Ray and Chip the dog behind them.

One man and his dog had saved the day for us as the hundreds of wild Achill sheep, with my two errant ewes leading the way, were where we wanted them.

Helen Calvey grew up producing Achill Mountain Lamb with her family in Mayo. Married with two children, she now lives in Galway where she is a regional manager with Siemens Healthcare and runs a pony and sheep farm in Connemara.

35 The Cockerel

Patricia Finn

HE always strutted around the hen-run with an air of superiority; he was the undisputed boss. As a three year old, however, I did not understand the role that he played.

It was a lovely sunny afternoon and I was outside playing with my dolls in the garden beside the hen run. I decided to go inside to watch the hens dust-bathing. I was intrigued by such an activity as I was under the impression that bathing should be done in water not in turf-mould. However, that was how they had their bath.

I was so busy watching the hens bathing and the little birds eating, sitting down on my hunkers taking it all in that I didn't notice the big Rhode Island Red cockerel approaching me.

He made a dive at me, landing so close that even though he was standing sideways, his beady eye still met my own two. I tried to stand up but as I did so he leaped at me. He started pecking at the ribbon in my hair and at my face near my eyes almost at the same time. I tried to throw him off but he just ended up drawing blood from my hands. I screamed at the top of my voice, hoping that someone would come to my aid.

The more I screamed, the louder and louder the cockerel shrieked.

My mother finally came running into the hen run with a stick and took a swipe at the cockerel.

He fled.

She picked me up and took me back into the house, dried my tears and wiped away the blood from the scrape-marks on my face and hands. She combed my hair and assured me that the cockerel would never bother me again.

I was feeling rather sorry for myself and so I went into my parents' bedroom to see the damage with my own eyes. Even though I was very small. I knew that the mirror on their dressing table was at my level and so I could see what the nasty cockerel had done to me.

What I didn't know was that when you looked at yourself in this particular mirror and moved quickly, it would distort the reflection. The person I saw staring back shocked me. Not only were there scratches but my entire face had changed shape completely. It was long and rather strange looking, a bit like the donkey that was in the field next to the house.

It was soon teatime, and I was called to come down to the table and join in the evening meal. When I joined the rest of them I asked if my face would ever be better again. My mother said that it would heal within a day or two.

I told them that I just didn't want to look like a donkey, and both my mother and Granny looked rather surprised and asked what I meant. I told them that I looked in the mirror in the dressing table and all that I could see was a very long face that didn't look like me at all, and that the cockerel had changed the look of my face forever. They burst out laughing, my granny said that the mirror had a bevelled edge and distorted the images that it reflected, so I didn't see myself as I really was.

That was all I needed to hear to reassure me. My mother said that she was more concerned about the cockerel attacking me than the image I saw in the mirror. Granny got her little mirror from her handbag after tea so I saw then that

I still looked like me. I was very happy with that outcome, no donkey-face to be seen.

Meanwhile there must have been a decision made on the part of my mother and Granny that I was not aware of as to the future of the cockerel.

Out playing the next day, I noticed that he was not in the hen run. When Granny came out to feed the hens, I asked where he was. She said he had died the previous night.

A few days later, I saw him hanging up in the shed without any feathers, his eyes closed and his beak shut. On the Sunday, I got the smell of chicken coming from our little black cooker.

My mother told me that we were having a roast dinner and she had made some stuffing balls to serve with it and roast potatoes too. When I asked her if it was the same bird that had attacked me, she confirmed it was. At that moment, my stomach heaved and the thoughts of eating the rooster I once knew revolted me.

Even as a three-and-a-half year old. I felt there was an injustice done to the cockerel. The dinner was served up to everyone, nicely presented on willow-pattern plates. All I could do was wish for it to be over. I prodded and poked at the meat on my plate, but I could not eat the poor old cockerel.

My mother just gave me potatoes and vegetables instead. I felt I owed my nemesis that much in death even if we hadn't seen eye to eye in life.

Patricia Finn is a housewife and Montessori teacher from Ballinabrackey, Co Meath. Married with two teenage boys, she enjoys walking, cycling, singing in the local folk choir and writing.

36 The Cow That Went On Holidays

Pat O'Dwyer

A NUMBER of years ago I was looking at old photos of our family with my aunt Essie who, at the time, was in her 80s. She was the only member of my dad's family still alive. The photos we were looking at were taken in the 1920s when my dad was about six years old and the youngest of five children.

Their father, Joe, was a well-known cattle dealer who used to attend many of the fairs around Tipperary, Limerick and Clare to buy cattle. He would then travel each Thursday by train to the great Dublin cattle fair off the North Circular road on Prussia Street.

As we were looking at these old photos, I was asking my aunt to tell me who the people were and what she could remember about each scene. Then we came across a photo of all the family at Limerick Junction getting ready to board a train to Dublin.

The five children, including my dad and Essie were all dressed up in their best outfits, smiling and looking very happy. With them were two ladies wearing long dresses and wide hats fashionable in that period.

My aunt told me the story of the picture: "We were going on our annual holiday to Dun Laoghaire for the month and the two ladies in the photo were our nannies. And Alice came too," she said with a big chuckle.

Not understanding I asked: "What do you mean Alice came too."

"Alice was our cow," she explained like it was the most natural thing in the world for a cow to take the train from Limerick Junction to Dun Laoghaire for its summer holidays with a family.

For a second I thought that aunt Essie was either playing a trick on me or time was playing a trick on her memory. On seeing the look of bewildered confusion on my face, she went on to say that Alice was sent on holiday with them to provide milk for the family for the month. She said that her father had rented an acre of grassland near to where they were staying for the month.

My aunt told me why the cow was so special to the family.

"When Alice was born she was a very unusual animal. Her mother, a Jersey breed, rejected her at birth so Alice was adopted by another cow. Because of her huge brown eyes and the way she would look at you, we named her 'Alice in Wonderland' but very soon she became just Alice.

"She was a very unusual colour, a sort of creamy gold and as a calf she became a real pet, often standing at the gate sucking one of our fingers.

"Alice grew up on the farm and remained a gentle animal. The older children could cuddle her, swing from her neck or venture in or out under her or even pull her tail. She never showed signs of aggression.

"The smaller children would whisper stories and secrets to her. At the age of two she became a mother herself and went on to have a calf every year for a long number of years. Being a Jersey, her milk was very creamy and was used in the house – it could be two to three inches thick with cream and was a favourite for our porridge.

"When we were going on holidays we would insist on Alice coming too. On the train when the ticket inspector came around to punch the tickets, we would have great fun with him saying: 'Where is Alice, we can't see her?'"

"Knowing full-well what the children were up to the ticket inspector would go off pretending to look for a little girl named Alice and would return saying: 'I can't find her, she must have been left behind at the station.'"

"We would all laugh saying she is on the train in the cow compartment," The inspector would say: 'What is a little girl doing in the cattle carriage?' and then we would tell him: 'Alice is a cow.' Gales of laughter would erupt from us and everybody sitting nearby. The same game was played each year with different ticket collectors.

"Alice lived until she was about 16 and when she died my father refused to have her taken away to be used for dog meat as was the custom, but buried her on the farm alongside other pets."

Essie finished her story and in the silence that followed, I could sense the fondness in her for the cow Alice even after 70 years. I asked how the cow got from Kingsbridge to Dun Laoghaire. "The drover," she replied. She explained that Alice was brought from the station to Dun Laoghaire by a drover her father knew from attending the weekly fair on Prussia Street.

At a time when holidays for families were few and far between, Alice was indeed unique – a cow who went on annual holidays.

Patrick O'Dwyer hails from Tipperary town, is in car sales and married with three children. He likes to collect and listen to stories about the land, past farm life and in particular old farm implements.

37 The Milking Parlour

Pauline Brew

IGREW up on a dairy farm where we had a lot of cows. As children, we all had our favourites among them. We had names for them and considered them our pets. However there was one huge disadvantage to having a large dairy herd because they had to be milked morning and evening and it took four or five people to do it.

They ruled our lives. No matter what time you got to bed you still had to be up at six in the morning for the milking. In the summer time when we went for a rare day out to the seaside, we had to be back by four in the afternoon to start the milking. I remember my mother saying: "It must be great to be a townie when you can come home whenever you like."

Then one day my father came from the town full of excitement about a new method of milking cows in a milking parlour.

He thought this would be ideal for us, as it would save us time and it would also be much more hygienic. After much talk, he decided to build the parlour and buy a milking machine.

A site was selected at the side of the big yard and over a few months the new building went up. It consisted of 10 stalls where the cows would stand during milking. Beside each stall was a pit where the person milking stood. From there you attached the clusters to the cow. The milk flowed along the pipes and went down to the end where it was collected in a tankard.

While we were all full of enthusiasm, the cows did not see it in quite the same way. The first evening we went to bring them in they went wild around the yard.

It took weeks to train them in. We started with the quieter ones and coaxed them with hay to get them to climb the step to the stalls.

We talked gently to them and then eased on the milking machine. Slowly, they lost their fear of it. After a while we succeeded in getting the others to follow suit.

We cordoned off a section of the yard with an electric fence to stop the wilder ones from getting away. Finally, things settled down.

The milking parlour became a part of our everyday farming routine. It was so easy to use. I spent one summer standing in the pit doing the milking; the machine did most of the work and I sang all the pop songs of the time.

The milking parlour was new and labour saving and we embraced its modernity. Who wouldn't when you could serenade the cows while the machine did all the hard work?

Pauline Brew grew up on a farm near Charleville, Co Cork but now lives in Limerick. Married with three children and four grandchildren, she is retired and enjoys writing as a hobby.

I was about to offer seconds when my father walked in with a young man I hadn't seen before. Sometimes the contractors have sons with them or young lads driving the tractors so I nodded at them to take their seats and served up two more plates. The young man's blue eyes widened as he looked at the plate of food.

'Is that for me?' he asked.

'Yes,' I replied somewhat surprised and as an afterthought, I added 'Enjoy.'

He did. He tucked in with gusto and a smile on his face.

I cleared away plates making a mental note to be less generous with the vegetables in the casseroles the next time. Some left carrots and some didn't like mushrooms, but the peas and onions seemed to be popular.

I noticed the young man was clearing his plate.

As I served rhubarb crumble and hot custard, the men started chatting. With bellies full, their tongues and brains could work in tandem so they compared notes and news. As the dessert bowl was placed in front of each man, he glanced at it as if suspicious of the contents and then relaxed slightly.

All except the young guy: his eyes widened further and his mouth broke into a wide grin as he tucked in. Was he a silent type, I wondered as I scalded the teapot? None of the other men seemed to be talking to him whereas they usually teased children and teenagers. However, he seemed happy enough as he drank tea and ate slices of biscuit cake. My biscuit cake was the only thing they all seemed happy to see.

As they supped the last dregs of tea from the mugs, the driver of the harvester stood up – the signal their dinner break was over. The men got to their feet and grunted a thank you as they went out. Was I imagining it or was there an implied 'thank goodness we won't be back again for a while'?

All apart from the teenager, who smiled and thanked me profusely. If he was a new member of staff, I hoped his enthusiasm would rub off on the others in time.

There was no sign of the lad at teatime. The men seemed happy that I was serving up a fry of sausages, rashers, baked beans and fried eggs – not a vegetable in sight.

'Where's the young man?' I enquired.

No one knew. Nor did any of them know who he was. He had walked down to where they were cutting silage on the outfarm. A school kid bored and on his summer holidays, he'd asked for a jaunt on a tractor and the driver had left him sitting on it when going in for dinner. Whether he didn't want him to suffer my cooking or didn't want to impose on my hospitality I'm not sure, but when my dad saw him sitting there he presumed he was one of the contractor's sons and insisted he 'come in for a bit of dinner'. Never could a person be left in the yard while dinner was being served inside. The rest of the contractors, seeing him come in with my dad, had presumed he was a visitor of ours. After they had finished drawing in silage from the outfarm, he had headed home.

To this day, I still don't know who it was that sat at my dinner table that hot summer's day and tucked into my cooking like it was the best he had ever tasted. At least I lived up to the tradition of hospitality, even if only one person really appreciated it.

Lorna Sixsmith farms in Co Laois with her husband and their two children. She is the author of two books: 'Would You Marry A Farmer?' and 'How To Be A Perfect Farm Wife'.

39 The Vixen And The Pup

Jack Byrne

MANY years ago, I had a truly wonderful Wicklow Collie Sheepdog called Shep. He was one of those exceptional dogs a man will only come across once in his lifetime. He was unusual in that he was grey and had a chainy-eye (one a different colour to the other). He was quite headstrong when I started training him but showed great promise from the word go and would let nothing away.

We had 17 acres rented outside Rathdrum all in one field. I used to bring him there in the evening and very soon he became really biddable, improving in leaps and bounds every time we practised.

My world fell apart when Shep picked up poison; I brought him to the vet and I stayed up all night with him but alas, he died three hours later. He was three and a half years old and struck down just as he was reaching his peak.

I was heartbroken.

Luckily, we had a collie bitch which had gone in pup by my good dog. One cold frosty March morning I looked into the kennel and there was a litter of five pups. Among them was a gorgeous grey pup and I was thrilled to discover that one had a chainy eye. I was so charmed with this pup, that I used to look in at it every time I passed by.

About ten days passed and one morning I checked and the pup was gone. I searched everywhere. It couldn't be found high up or low down.

My world fell apart once again. It really puzzled me because the bitch was tied up except when she was working so she couldn't have moved it.

The end of March and April came and the ewes had their lambs and I had them on rented land. By the second week in May we had the lambs earmarked, tailed, castrated etc. It had rained heavily the night before and the day was just brightening up. I gathered up the ewes and lambs and was working with them through a bushy and boggy area.

Out of the blue I thought I could hear a yelp but wasn't sure because of the din the ewes and lambs were making. I thought I had heard it somewhere in the bushes and when I moved the sheep a bit away I went back to listen again; sure enough I heard another yelp.

I got down on my hands and knees and clambered through the bushes and rushes and my eyes nearly popped out of their sockets, when I saw my missing pup. He was wet and bedraggled looking from the rain, but I was surprised at how heavy he looked.

I can only conclude that a vixen stolel him and fed him as her own. There is no doubt that it would have been unable to fend for itself as it was only 10 days old when it disappeared.

He turned out a wonderful dog and I had him working for me for many years.

Jack Byrne works on his sheep and dairy farm near Roundwood, Co Wicklow, where he was born and reared. Married with three children and seven grandchildren, he enjoys set dancing and recitations.

40 A Quiet Christmas

Bunty Flynn

I LOVED the Christmas cards from America that came to my Grandmother's house. Some were shaped like Christmas trees and had pictures of fat red Daddy Christmases and cute robins on sprigs of holly and had a sparkly dust that fell on the scrubbed deal kitchen table.

She was my mother's mother and for as far back as I can remember she wore black. She was a widow on a small fertile farm and had produced 10 children and had seen four of them off to America from Cobh, then known as Queenstown.

When I was small she seemed like a giant sitting with her back ramrod straight in the back-to-back trap her knees covered with a faded black rug. I sat with my back to hers jammed in between my aunts as my uncle steered Sally, the chestnut mare, over the white dusty road to Mass.

She liked her garden, which she had made in the yard in front of the long thatched house, which she had fenced in with small hexagon lettuce wire to keep the Rhode Island reds out.

On the right hand corner of the thatched roof grew a cluster of succulents, which she called 'hens and chicks.' These brought luck to a house, she said. Swallows too were lucky and each May she looked out for the first pair to swoop and shriek as they flew into the cow house or pigsty.

She fed the roses with manure, the older the better my grandmother said. Manure was like good wine it matured and got better with age. She also covered the roots with crushed egg -shells and threw used water from the dishes to keep them moist and to keep off greenfly.

As summer turned to autumn, late evening would see her head bent, her nose buried in the remaining few roses as she hummed 'The Last Rose of Summer.'

The Rosary was said each night, all members of the family on their knees except my Grandmother. She would sit like a black Madonna fingering her black beads until the final hurdle, which was the Hail Holy Queen. At this my uncles would shift their knees restlessly on the hard stone floor, knowing only too well that the trimmings were still ahead.

Prayers for family, absent family, for neighbours, for friends and for good weather or sometimes for rain, and finally for daughter Nell in New York that she would soon be cured and re-united with her husband and two young girls.

Then after hot milk or cocoa she retired to bed, a candle in one hand and her walking cane in the other. She'd draw the blind and then shake holy water with green palm over me and over the large feather bed.

Her grey bun was then untied and her hair hung down her back in a plait tapering to a thin wisp at the end. Some times a moth or a daddy-long-legs would flit around the ceiling and she would try to remove them with her stick. She had no problem swatting moths but daddy-long-legs were lucky creatures, she said.

Every morning she eagerly awaited the visit of the postman longing for a letter or a parcel from America. One day a letter came from Nell and contained a photo of her standing in a long dressing gown on the sunny veranda of a sanatorium.

"Isn't it a lovely place, Granny?" I enthused but with

pursed lips and a shake of her head she replied: "Wisha child, good to have but bad to want." Sanatorium was a word that I did not understand.

She was always serene except when she beat the heads from the buachaláns in the orchard field. Yellow devils she called them. The law forbad the growth of these and there was a hefty fine then, 'Free State how are you' she would rail.

Although she did little real work, she did sew sheets together on the old Singer foot machine from flour bags, the red writing having been first bleached out of them as they hung to dry in the orchard. She kept buttons and string in old jam jars and darned socks using a wooden mushroom and a large darning needle. She recycled out of necessity.

Among the jobs she delegated to me was bringing in the eggs in the old bucket like basket. She inspected and counted them and then wrote how many I had brought in an old black notebook. When the egg man came she carefully counted the coins he had paid her and placed them in her deep apron pocket.

I was taken with her as she followed the path by the graveyard in search of the first sound of the cuckoo. We'd enter and pray for all the cousins and with her stick she would poke the glossy ivy on the corner of the ruined church gable to reveal the carved stone face of a saint or monk. Should we happen to see a single magpie she would make the sign of the cross and say "Good day, Mr. Magpie." I'd be instructed to "keep my eyes peeled for another one" as two were for joy.

On May eve she went to the animals and sprinkled them with holy water holding a lit wax candle. She also liberally sprinkled the four corners of the yard and I got a liberal amount of the splashes as I followed in her wake.

In early December, if the weather permitted we would go

on the look out for holly to decorate the Christmas candle. My uncle was sent to cut the most berried holly from the higher branches.

It was a mild December the year the boy came from town with the telegram. She was expecting the usual bundle of Christmas cards, but none came that morning.

My grandmother read and re-read the green page and then folded the telegram and with her knobbly fingers, picked the petals from a pink translucent rose and carefully placed them in the envelope with the telegram, tears flowing into the wrinkles on her ashen face.

TB had had yet again claimed another victim... her daughter. There were no Christmas cards from America that year.

Bunty Flynn is a retired Play School Teacher, lives in Mitchelstown, Co Cork is married with three children and four grandchildren. She is a member of a Writer's Group and her hobbies are writing short stories and playing golf.

41 The Cows' Highway

Sandra Coffey

TRACKS have always fascinated me. I'd wonder where a track came from and where it led. I'd follow it with my eyes and imagine the comings and goings that would race across it. My fascination with tracks began during my farming childhood where I woke every morning to watch a herd of cows make their way across the fields on their own well-beaten tracks.

Large green-boxed areas of grass were fenced in by single and double stonewalls. Across them was their track. The cows moved between the fields as they made their way through the day. You could tell by the track what route they took, swerving only a little to left or right before straightening up again.

It was on this same track, the one I saw from my bedroom window, that I learnt how to ride a bicycle and I'd invite friends over to cycle on the 'Cows' Road' as we called it.

My bedroom window overlooked the milking parlour and as the cows made their way to its entrance, I was ready to help with the mornings milking before I boarded the bus to school. When I got to the age where I could help with the milking, I was allowed a pet. Lisa was my cow's name. Although she was only five years old, she had already given birth three times. One of those times there was great excitement as she had twins, quite a rarity on our farm.

I remember my dad saying to me: "You've picked the best

cow on the farm", as we watched her place her feet carefully onto the concrete and take up her position for milking. I smiled thinking I knew a good cow when I saw one even if I was only nine.

We never had any need to check the time in our house; when the cows arrived, we knew it was half seven. It was like the cows had a secret code among them. One would lift its body off the grass leaving behind a solitary dry patch. Then the next... and the next.

Slowly, they would make their way along the track already marked out by their own feet from the previous day. Sometimes a rogue cow would mark out its own path only to find in time its place among the herd. They'd march in a single file and wait for us at the destination.

Same again that evening; same again the following day.

It was the same cow that led the way every time. She was mainly white with black patches but her face had a black patch over her left eye. We nicknamed her Popeye.

Looking at their bursting udders, I wondered at the weight of all that milk and how they would carry it to us twice a day and head off happily after leaving it behind.

I closed the gate behind the herd and watched as the cows made their own way back to the green fields, walking along their track. I smiled and wondered if I was the only girl in the area who enjoyed such a simple yet wondrous work of nature.

The next day was heavy with rain and the track was muddy and slippery. I noticed that a track had petered off the main track and it roused my curiosity. As the cows made their way through the milking, we realised we were missing one. Dad's worry came bubbling to the surface in a rush across his face.

"Where is she?" he asked. "I hope she's okay."

Once the milking was finished, we turned on the cooling system and headed off across the fields. We too used the track and followed in a single file behind the cows that walked ahead of us. The nerves in my stomach were rising as I thought of all the bad things that could happen. We followed the new track up to the corner of the field. The cow was lying down.

Dad said: "She looks okay. But what is she doing up here?"

The cow barely moved as we approached, chewing her cud and catching the first waves of sunshine that were breaking through.

Dad walked around her and I could tell he had seen something as his face changed from worry to a huge toothy grin.

Behind the cow was a bitch and her new litter of puppies. Not a drop of rain had fallen on them. The cow had shielded them from the elements and the certain night-time dangers that would have been attracted to the scent of freshly-born animals.

"Look at this," he said, gesturing to me to come over for a look.

I couldn't believe it, there was five puppies all snuggled together like piglets nestling under their mother.

In the weeks that followed, the dog and her puppy would every day visit the cow that helped them that night. I'd watch as they'd sidle over and walk the fields with her until they came back home in the evening. The other cows seemed to welcome them too.

"You can learn so much from animals and what they do for each other," said Dad.

◆　　◆　　◆

My bedroom window remains but the view has changed utterly. The tracks too are different. The dual carriageway beneath can't take people to their destination fast enough.

I imagine these lanes joining up with many others like a puzzle reaching out to connect with its other pieces. School buses are so clean you could tell they never saw a country road. Cats' eyes and the sounds of urban life scratch their way into country fields where once our cows tracked their way to and from the fields for milking.

Sandra Coffey is a native of Co Galway where she grew up on a farm. She enjoys writing fiction and lives in Galway.

42 The Spailpín

Mary O'Connor

NED was a spailpín – a wandering farm labourer – who arrived at gran's farm at the end of every autumn.

The imminence of his annual appearance was usually predicted fairly accurately by grandad and preparations for his stay were duly implemented.

He timed his arrival to coincide with the harvesting of the potatoes and the increased chores of foddering the cattle. He waited until the threshing was over and the 'meitheal' were home on their farms for he was a loner and never worked with others or participated in conversation.

His accommodation was in the garage with its white washed walls, cement floor and electric light. The car was moved to another location for the duration and a cast-iron bed was erected, the mattress and bedclothes aired. A rope mat was placed beside the bed and a table, chair, basin, towels and a big bar of red carbolic soap left on a saucer.

A small mirror, purchased from the travelling woman Mrs Kiely hung on the wall and couple of red paper flowers, purchased from the same source, sat in a jam jar with the aim of enhancing the appearance of Ned's bedroom.

Grandad prepared the room and there was a general prohibition on anyone looking in or attempting to go near the door at any time while Ned was staying there.

Nobody was sure where Ned hailed from but it was thought it was somewhere in Co. Laois and that he was born in a workhouse. I witnessed his arrival once when I was on a weekend visit. Gran looked out the kitchen window and said: 'Well, well, here's poor Ned.' I stood on my tippy-toes and saw a burly man in his fifties walk up the tree-lined avenue towards the farmhouse. He was dressed in a coarse grey suit, with a grey muffler wrapped around his neck and a grey cap pulled down over one eye. It was said that he did this because he had a 'cast'. He had a bundle under his arm and wore hob-nailed boots that had picked up the dust of the roads.

He came to the back door and Gran said: "God bless you Ned, you're welcome" and invited him in to the kitchen. She sat him down at the table beside the window and we went out to the dairy where she cut a few thick rashers of home-cured bacon. I was assigned the task of taking in a dish of homemade butter and a jug of milk that were also kept there as it was almost like a cold room and had been purpose built.

She took a couple of her free range eggs from the dresser in the back kitchen and put the pan on the cream Rayburn cooker with its turf fire blazing. She then cut several slices of her home made soda-bread, 'wet' the tea in the brown delph teapot and served the sizzling fry to Ned.

Gran and I remained in the back kitchen where she explained that he was a bit 'odd' and liked to dine alone. She also said that he talked to himself quite a lot. When he was finished, Grandad walked with Ned to his quarters across the front yard where they discussed the farm work to be done and, no doubt, the financial arrangements.

I never saw Ned working at his various chores on the

farm. He was only ever visible at meal times. Ned dined alone after the rest of the family had eaten and did not engage in conversation. No questions were asked and therefore no questions had to be answered.

He sat at the kitchen table in the same place beside the window with his back to the range, while the rest of the family adjourned to the back kitchen. Every morning with the exception of Fridays, he partook of a plate of rashers, eggs and fried bread. On Fridays a couple of eggs were boiled.

At dinner time there was a big meal of home cured bacon, turnips or cabbage and boiled potatoes. On Fridays, Gran made colcannon and fried eggs. The evening meal usually consisted of cold bacon and scallions or an onion with lashings of soda bread and 'country' butter while cheese or eggs were the usual Friday fare. After supper Gran gave Ned a mug of milk and home baked currant bread to take to his quarters.

After a couple of months Grandad usually recognised the symptoms of Ned's pending departure. He would become restless as his feet itched for the road again and he would spend two or three days looking up at the sky. One morning Grandad would go out and notice the garage door bolted on the outside. That meant that Ned had gone.

No one ever saw him leave. Ned had answered the 'glaoch an bhóthair,' which led him God knows where – alone, always alone as he tramped the bleak bogroads of Offaly and Laois in wind and rain, alone with his thoughts, alone with his memories, and his fate.

One late autumn Grandad made the usual preparations in the garage for Ned's anticipated arrival, but the bedclothes on the cast-iron bed remained undisturbed that year.

Some time later Grandad heard that Ned had died that winter in the County Home... alone, as he had lived.

Mary O'Connor is a PhD legal researcher at Queens University Belfast. She lives in Edenderry, Co Offaly and is interested in history and literature.

43 The Maypole

Johnny Flynn

I AM not that old for history lessons but I'm old enough to dance though. The people in the house have just finished their dinner.

Earlier we were at Sunday Mass in the Church at Ballinamuck. This village is small with a hall with the Pike man on a stand outside the Post Office and the pub. I do not understand when people speak of '98 but this memorial means a lot to them.

We are now going to walk to the 'Nailors.' So come along with me on the road. The attire of the pike man looks queer to me as we pass on the way but who cares. We bless ourselves as we pass the church and head for the '98 bar – a thatched low house between two roads and the sharp hill of one of them.

Beyond the hedge I notice the whins with their heathery colour and hear the birds sing; I too sing silently. Crossing the hill we leave Longford for lovely Leitrim. My heart soars as others on bikes pass by.

Going downhill we run by Mary Ellen's and miss the smell of her flowers in the front garden. I can hear the music now and it's not too far, we're close to the crossroads that gets its name from Mick the Nailors, who fashioned nails.

The Maypole is in the garden at the back of the house and safe for children. It was a timber construction placed on the grass an imitation of a small dance hall without a roof. No need for lights as this is happening at three in the afternoon.

Our enthusiasm to dance banished our coyness and with or without shoes we took to the floor. The musicians like us are local with a fiddle and accordion.

I meet Liz who grew up at the crossroads and told me about the names on the four roads and what they meant. One was 'Nannies Road' called after a respected, wise older woman. The 'Newline Road' led to church and the school called Drumgowna. The 'High Road' was for fun and frolic and 'The Far Town road' was the one I've just journeyed on.

Simple ways.

Simple days.

The sheer joy of meeting friends and being part of a crowd. People there knew me and bought me something in the small shop in front of the garden.

Most of the adults stayed out on the Cross playing skittles or just talking.

This was a day when we were somewhere over the rainbow. And it did not rain that Sunday.

Then the time came for us to go home and we retraced our steps.

That was years and years ago and today I find myself faraway, in distance and age but always retracing my steps to the first Maypole, which is as alive in me as if it happened only yesterday.

John Flynn comes from Leitrim village where he farms along with his wife. He likes to champion the cause of all things Leitrim at local and national level.

44 Achtung... Lights, Camera And Action

Gretta Tynan

WE woke up very early that morning, me and my older brother Oliver. He was nine years old and I was four. Jeff, our pet pig had slept soundly between the two of us since Oliver had taken pity on him the night before. Reluctantly we stayed in the bed for a little while even though we were bursting with excitement.

Finally, the Germans were coming to our farm. We were going to be on German television.

Daddy and Mammy and all of us were part of a programme on life on a small farm in Ireland. "Now Colm," my brother said, "we just have to figure out what to do with Jeff today."

Oliver had a plan to make Jeff famous, even if it was in Germany. He picked up the piglet, gave him a kiss, and said: "We're gonna be famous someday." The pig squealed a little and wagged his butty tail as if in agreement.

When we heard the hum of the milking machine we jumped up and put Jeff in a trunk in our bedroom. We left the lid open a tiny bit to allow him to breathe because that would be his home for the remainder of the morning.

Something strange had happened to our kitchen overnight. It was tidier than usual, but everything looked a different colour, even the sky blue walls appeared green! Charlie, my father, was sitting at the table eating his porridge.

He had his Sunday clothes on and he looked more tanned than usual.

"God bless the work, my good men", he said. Mam stood at the range mashing an egg in a cup. She wiped her brow and swept back her thick brown hair saying: "I hope you boys have left your room tidy". Her blue pinafore with the yellow daisies appeared to be orange. I noticed that all the windows were covered with orange plastic film – it was like living inside a Lucozade bottle. Charlie explained that this was supposed to block out some of the sunlight for the camera man and it would be gone next week.

A huge black transit van arrived with strange looking number plates. Max, our German shepherd, who was used to lots of vehicles coming and going as there were eleven in our family, barked non-stop for five minutes. Oliver and I watched intently as a tall, dark haired man emerged from the van.

We had never seen a German before and didn't know quite what to expect. His strong arms carefully unloaded something that looked like a big telescope, a tripod and huge lights. He was the camera man and his name was Otto. His broad smile put us at ease immediately.

In the distance, we could hear something rattling down the long lane to our house. It was our neighbour Neddy coming on his high nelly sailing majestically between potholes. "I wonder which of them this is now", said Mammy, as he shared the same bike and same Sunday suit with his equally nosey brother.

"I saw the hearse coming in your gate, and wondered who had died", Neddy blurted out.

"Not today, Thank God", replied my father. Neddy hopped off his bike and proceeded to light his pipe happy in the knowledge that all was well. Making himself at home he sat on the pier to watch proceedings.

Oliver and I decided this was a good time to sneak into our bedroom and feed some slops to Jeff. We wanted him in tip-top condition for his debut.

At that time Martin and Gerard, two of our older brothers, had just finished the milking and left the enamel bucket half full of lovely frothy milk at the scullery door. This, along with some crusts of bread, would do the trick.

By now, Otto and his fair-haired assistant Hans had set up all the equipment in our large kitchen. Mammy was preparing the dinner – a traditional one of bacon, cabbage and spuds (all homegrown, of course).

It was lights, camera and action. The temperature was rising with the Stanley range all fired up and the extra bright lights in every corner. It took about four hours to cook from start to finish. Hunger was getting the better of us but at least it gave us time to plan our next move.

We discovered a few months before quite by accident that our pig had a habit of bobbing his snout up and down continuously when he fell into a bucket of salt. He persisted in nodding for at least five minutes. It dawned on us that this could be turned into a talent. I had just got a small keyboard from Santa at Christmas. Oliver said: "Let's try this just once".

So he got the salt cellar and shook some on Jeff's nose. Immediately, the pig began playing the keyboard brilliantly with some help from my brother.

This was the pig's party piece which we had managed to keep secret until now. We just couldn't wait to see everyone's reaction.

After dinner, Oliver brought Jeff out to the kitchen, and I had the keyboard and the salt. We had put a dickie bow on

Jeff and he looked like a star already. Mammy and Daddy exchanged baffled expressions. Jeff played: 'We All Live in a Yellow Submarine' with great stamina! Otto and Hans caught all the action on camera. We all joined in and sang along.

I can say now that I never saw my mother so shocked and delighted all at once. My father grinned and said proudly: "That was great teamwork boys, if only we can have the pig playing music while the cows are milking – it might improve the butterfat!"

In *The Farmers Journal* the following week the heading said:

'Small Pig is a Big Hit with the Germans'

It so happened that the day after the famous filming, the Farmers Journal reporter came to visit our farm and interviewed our parents. We were growing very accustomed to the spotlight, but no-one shone quite like Jeff, the first Irish pig to make it big in European television!

Gretta Tynan is a homemaker and farmer who hails from Granard in Co Longford. A secretary/special needs assistant by profession, she is married with 4 children.

45 The Race To The Bottom Of The World

Ciaran Condren

THE old yard was rectangular in shape, created 200 years earlier to house the horses of the yeomandry but was now a farmyard with the cowhouses on one side and the disused stables used for storage and housing cattle.

Right down one side of the yard was a drain and on a rainy day the water teemed unrestricted from the rusting galvanised roofs in great flows of abundance splashing the rough concrete yard below into a clean white line.

The outflow from the roofs meandered through the farmyard dirt and debris and joined the gushing drain that had been supplemented by the torrent of water thundering down the back lane and into the farm yard,

The confluence was manna from heaven for the imaginations of the two young boys who shared the farmyard with their family and the farm livestock. In those simpler days the islanders outlook to beyond the isle was enhanced by a feature of the education curriculum that allowed school kids to track Irish merchant ships around the globe.

There was regular feedback to the schools detailing what exotic port on the other side of the world the Irish Merchant vessels were berthed in. The positions were tracked on a massive wall map and each ship's representative marker was meticulously relocated as the intelligence on the ship was fed back to the wide-eyed 'explorers.'

The torrent of water tearing down the drain in the yard became a microcosm of the planet.

The wetter the day, the better the play. Short sticks two to three inches long were christened the Oak or the Sycamore (The ships were called after native tree species).They were then launched without much fanfare onto the raging torrent and a race to the other side of the world was set in train.

The world was reduced to a run of roughly 100 yards of a racing track. The launched ships would need encouragement to seek out their destination on the far side. At times they would catch onto unstoppable rapids and the 'captains' would barely be able to keep pace as they raced along splashing through the cow-dung and the dirty water in the incessant rain.

Other times misfortune would bedevil the gallant clippers and they would spin frustratingly out of a whirlpool into a backwater where they would twist and twirl in aimless despair as the competing bark dashed haughtily by. In this world, the captain had great licence to assist his stricken charge.

With a stick the 'captain' could prod his vessel and scrape away piles of cowdung or any other obstacle that was blocking the forward progress of his pride and joy. There were no rules other than that the ship could not leave the water.

Pride was at stake. The farmyard filled with screams and shouts and curses that ebbed and flowed with the fortunes of the vessels on the high seas. As the rainfall increased and the conditions got wilder we were no longer on an island on the edge of Europe but atop a masthead battling the savage conditions of the roaring forties.

The rainfall disappeared, the farmyard disappeared, the dung disappeared and the wild world of the high seas raced around in our heads. That lump of rock at the bottom of the yard where the stream turned abruptly east was Rio de Janiero where we reloaded at the bottom of the Atlantic before making the mad dash across to Australia.

That patch of still water where the flow eased and the ship lolled lazily was the airless tranquillity of the doldrums. How would any self-respecting captain permit his ship to wander in there? However there were times when things went wrong in the races and what could one do only admit defeat and resolve that it would not happen in the next race.

At the bottom of the world the waters gushed into a manhole and disappeared into a four inch red clay drainage pipe. Tremendous care was necessary to ensure that the carefully carved racing machine was rescued before it plunged into this unfathomable oblivion. It was whipped up and carefully examined especially if it had won. The captain then waited for the vanquished to arrive at the finishing point.

With a splashing dash to the top of the world it would all start again, and again and again while the rain lasted. The races always terminated with the arrival of milking time,

The lovely ladies of the dairy had no respect for world order but would stand patiently oblivious of the interruption that they were causing to our sporting lives. They frequently discharged regime changing deposits right in the channels of our raceways as they waited to be milked in the cow shed.

This time was often used to refuel for the after milking racing and the changing of our clothing as after a few hours we would be soaked to the skin.

Hours of our lives were dedicated to these honourable

pursuits and when the summer came we looked wistfully at the scant cloud cover sweeping westward without the faintest promise of a downpour.

As Autumn arrived our desire to see the rain grew increasingly. These new downpours overcame the capacity of the parched earth to absorb the rainfall and soon the drain running through the farm yard was filling rapidly again.

It was time for the dried out ships to be relaunched from their docks as a new season had begun.

Ciaran Condren lives on a farm with suckler cows and a dog in the Macamores in North Wexford. He is married with two teenage boys.

46 The Lion In The Lamb

Rhoda Twombly

IT is cold and wet outside with winds blowing a gale but a two-day old lamb is warming my feet. More specifically, a ram lamb, rejected at birth by his mother.

My sister-in-law Sheila, who lives a couple of hundred yards down the road, rang to say: "We have a very poorly lamb down here. Can you come and help?"

"Just finishing the dishes, I'll be down in a minute!" I answered, throwing the dishtowel on the counter and grabbing my jacket as I headed out the door.

When you live on a small island as we do, and your only neighbours are family, it is second nature to lend a hand. Our land is close to my brother-in-law Tom's cattle and sheep farm, so my partner Joe and I often assist during lambing and calving season.

Joe, Tom and their sister Sheila patrol at all hours during those times and often find lambs left alone or abandoned in the field. Inexperienced, first-time ewes will sometimes wander off, leaving their newborn behind. This time of year if the cold doesn't kill them, the fox will.

An abandoned lamb needs to be warmed and fed immediately so Sheila and I often act as surrogate mums. Many initially appear dead so it is always a joy when vigorous rubbing brings them to life. From the tone of Sheila's voice I knew to hasten my step.

I ran through the darkness, my torchlight wavering wildly on the road ahead, my untied laces nearly tripping me up. In two minutes I was in the family home. The new lamb, pillowed by a pile of towels, lay by the open fire.

My brother-in-law came in and stood warming his hands at the hearth. "Tom," I said, "this fellow must be a twin, he's so small. Did she have another lamb?"

"She did. I just found a second one in the field. That one is stronger and I brought her and the ewe into the barn for the night."

Tom found this lamb, now warming at his fire in a ditch where the ewe had left him, unwashed and very cold. I picked him up. He weighed nothing, a bit of stubby matted wool in my arms. Sheila handed me fresh towels and I started rubbing. And rubbing. And rubbing. His body did not yet fit his accordion-pleated skin and his still unopened eyes and drooping ears were not a good sign. However, his breathing was even and strong and I felt gentle heat radiate through the wool.

Sheila bustled out from the kitchen with a beaker of Survival – a substitute for the ewe's first milk, or beestings as it is known in these parts. Nutrient and antibody-rich, it is vital in the initial thriving of a mammal. Praying that this helpless creature was strong enough to swallow, I gently pried open his mouth and slowly fed him using a syringe. Most of it ended up on my trousers but I could feel his throat swallowing a drop or two.

Their 91-year old auntie stood next to my chair, tentatively patting the top of the trembling head, "Nice, doggie," she said. "Nice doggie." Auntie suffers from dementia and often mixes up animals. And food. And people. But her eyes lit up as she stroked the quivering bundle.

Tom returned from the barn after checking on the ewe and her other lamb with a surprised but pleased look on his face. "You'll never guess!" he exclaimed as he walked into the house, a cold draft at his heels.

"What?" I asked, looking up at him, smiling. The lamb in my lap had opened his eyes at last and was making an effort to lift his head.

"It's not twins – it's triplets! When I looked in at the barn, there it was, another lamb born."

Lamb triplets are relatively uncommon, but not especially rare. As I fed our patient another few drops of milk I thought about the unusually high number of triplets born on the island so far this year. There were five sets, if you counted the one set that, sadly, died in the ewe. I wondered if there would be more.

I kept rubbing, feeling the delicate bones tremble but the body becoming warmer. After about 45 minutes, just as Auntie was stroking his head, out came a soft, tentative, "baa". My shoulders relaxed; a lamb crying out is a sign of strength. The rubbing and small amounts of milk were doing their work, but I wasn't out of a job just yet.

"Will you bring him home with you?" asked Sheila. "Tom's worried the ewe might not manage to feed all three."

"I will, of course," I replied, gathering the mite to my chest, feeling the miniscule hooves start to weakly kick. As ewes have only two teats, feeding triplets can be troublesome, especially for first-time mothers.

Joe and I will bottle-feed this fellow for weeks. During the next few days, we'll watch the lamb closely to make sure his digestion is working properly, that he is peeing enough and doesn't develop scour (diarrhoea), a common illness in young sheep. As much as I dislike cleaning up after a young lamb, I hoped for plenty of dirty newspapers as I walked back to my house with the bundle in my arms.

As a lamb imprints on its caregiver, no doubt I'll find him underfoot on a regular basis. They are resilient creatures and this little fellow, named Pita (for Pain in the Ass) is showing all the signs of growing into a fine, healthy ram.

Looking at him now, this tiny lion in lamb's clothing draped across my feet, I marvel at the miracle of nature.

Rhoda Twombly lives on Inishlyre, a small island in Clew Bay, Co Mayo with her partner, two dogs and two cats as well as a small herd of cattle. She is secretary of 'Comhdháil Oileáin na hÉireann' and writes short stories and poetry.

47 The Long Grass

Maeve Edwards

I T is 1961 and the air is filled with the sounds of summer. We've spent the morning playing piggy beds, but have grown tired of it now and look around us for diversion. We gather on our wall and watch my mother as she clips the hedge around the garden.

The baby is in his pram, straining against his harness and yelling to be let out. He is golden with the sun and his hair flops down over one eye. We take turns pushing his pram up and down the street at high speed. "Go easy with him now," calls my mother as we race past her for the third time. At the end of the road, the boys are busy making go-carts. We watch them for a while as they hammer old roller skates onto the bottom of their carts, but this holds no interest for us and we wander back to the wall idly wondering what to do next.

"Why don't you catch bees?" suggests my mother and after a moment's dismissal, this idea takes root. Soon we are rummaging in the press under the sink, rinsing out old jam jars, finding lids that fit and stabbing holes in them with a knife.

The two-acre green opposite our house has become a meadow these past two months. The grass has grown long and we reach out and brush the feathery tips with the palms of our hands. The dog joins us, leaping along beside us as we pluck clover heads and buttercups, dropping them in the bottom of our jam jars. We spread out through the long grass, our eyes peeled for those black and yellow stripes, that first flutter of tiny wings.

Soon the shout goes up: "I've caught one. I've caught one!" We run back and peer into the jar. A huge bumblebee is buzzing around inside, his small body dancing furiously at his entrapment. We can hear his angry buzzing through the jar, muted but thrilling all the same. We examine him minutely, and search his tiny legs for that magical sac of honey, but this bumblebee didn't have time to build up a store before his capture.

We resume our slow meander through the long grass and before long, I have two, then three bees in my jar. I sit down to examine them but am distracted by the cuckoo spit which seems to be attached to every buttercup head around me. I poke the spit with a daisy stalk and find what I'm looking for – a luminous green froghopper in all his big eyed splendour.

We spy a ladybird crawling up a blade of grass and we clamour around him, longing to have him for ourselves. "I saw him first." We reach out to him and he obligingly walks from outstretched finger to outstretched finger. And then my mother is there beside us, carrying the baby, and instructing us to mind him while she finishes clipping the hedge.

Soon the ladybird opens his strange wings and takes flight, leaving us with a feeling of sadness. We open our jam jars and toss the contents out onto the flattened grass. The bumblebees take a minute to recover, crawling over the limp clover heads before finding their wings, and flying away, high up into the sky.

The following morning we are called from sleep by the unmistakable sound of a tractor. I run down the stairs, holding my nightdress high above my knees. I fling open the front door, and shout back up the stairs: "Get up quick. He's here. The grass cutting man is here!" We race through our breakfast, barely able to suppress our excitement. "Take your time," says my mother. You won't be allowed onto the green until that man has cut every last blade of grass!"

Soon, we children are lined up along our wall drumming our heels and watching the drama unfold before our eyes. Backwards and forwards across our two acre green plods the grass cutting man on his tractor. The sweet scent of the cut grass mesmerises us and for one glorious moment, we are farm children, pitchforks in hand, ready to help with the haymaking.

By lunchtime, we are given the all clear. By now hordes of us have gathered and we descend, whooping and clapping, onto the green. We gather up armfuls of cut grass, enormous sweet smelling heaps of it and pile them high in a circle. All around us the other children are doing the same until a village of grass huts grows before our eyes, sprung up like mushrooms after rain.

Round and round we build until the smaller children grow tired and refuse to gather anymore. Soon our grass huts are finished and we sit inside in the green gloom, absorbing the intoxicating scent, our knees scuffed, our socks green with grass juice. Mothers come out on doorsteps to call us in for our tea, but we cannot leave our grass huts. We just cannot. "Can we have it out here? Oh Please!"

By evening, we are tired of peacefully sitting inside our grass huts and begin to cast glances at our neighbours. What if we were to organise a raiding party and steal their grass! As if by some osmosis, the message is passed from grass hut to grass hut and soon our park is a heave of children shouting and raiding and laughing, until our grass huts are no more. But this too wanes and soon we are called in for bed, and ordered to sit on the side of the bath and scrub the grass stains from our feet.

Building our huts each morning and tearing them down in the evening becomes the pattern of our days. By the end of the week, the grass has lost its moist lustre and soon the man who cut it is back with his horse and cart. He looks around him with satisfaction at the two acres of child turned hay before him.

"It'll feed him for the winter," he says as he forks it onto the back of his cart. We take turns patting the horse and marvelling at the perfection of it all.

Maeve Edwards is originally from Clontarf but now lives in Bray, Co Wicklow. A mother of two, she was shortlisted for a Hennessy Award in 2012.

48 The Country Shop

Michael Lynch

WHEN I go into a supermarket now, I just can't believe the number of items you can purchase, some of which you would not know what they are for. Back in the mid-forties, during the 'Emergency' I was dispatched regularly to a little country shop owned by two brothers, Jemmie and Johnny, mostly for bread, tea and sugar.

Most foods were rationed and tea and sugar were particularly hard to get. Each family had a ration book with coupons which the shopkeeper tore out when you got your ration.

Fortunately, Jemmie and Johnny didn't bother too much with the coupons. I don't know how they were able to get the food but they seemed to have a lot of contacts.

People would come from far and wide looking for a few cigarettes, a loaf of bread or paraffin oil. Jemmie stayed at home in the shop all day – he never went to Mass, meeting or church, and he did all the cooking. He would boil four big duck eggs, two huge mugs of tea and four rounds of a loaf. It was more or less the same every day.

He kept most of the items he sold in their kitchen. They stacked the batch loaves on the kitchen table, the paraffin oil in the 40 gallon barrel on the kitchen floor and the bag of flour in the corner of one side of the fire with the big bag of sugar on the other side.

There was no hygiene laws back then which was lucky for the dog as he was always curled up on top of the bag of sugar. In fact when Jemmie needed to fill sugar for you, he would shout at the dog to get him off the bag.

The tea came in a teachest – a plywood box lined with tinfoil. When he was selling you a few ounces of tea he'd tear half a page of a newspaper and turn it into a little cone shape packet in which to hold the tea.

The women were forever looking for the empty teachest to use as a play pen for a young child. They would also ask him to keep the empty flour bags so that they could make nappies for their babies.

The other brother, Johnny, had the travelling shop with a jennet and cart. He travelled the roads for miles on end buying eggs and chickens and selling a small amount of groceries to the people he bought from. Mostly he operated a barter system. Johnny walked behind the cart most of the time so as not to overload the poor old animal. Every night he came home with sore feet and rubbed butter on his toes and got the dog to ease the aches by licking his feet.

Jemmie and himself plucked all the chickens he bought up on his travels that day. There could be up to three dozen, all hanging upside down, on a line in the shed until the lorry from Dundalk arrrived to pick them up.

Jemmie kept the cigarettes and tobacco down in the room because if people knew he had them the whole country would arrive at his door. People went out of their mind for a smoke.

He had 'loose' cigarettes in a box of 500 and would just take a few out of the box and hand them to you. There were many brands at the time– Sweet Afton, John Player, Gold Flake, Wild Woodbine. Wild Woodbine were the cheapest to buy but

not very nice to smoke. Still, they were better than nothing and you could buy them in little packets of four for two pence. There was also another rare brand called Craven A and Blackcat.

He sold pipe tobacco and chewing tobacco. The pipe tobacco came in a solid bar about two inch square. He cut it up in two ounce lumps and that's the way it was sold. The other tobacco was called 'pigtail' which many old men chewed on.

A simple country shop that had everything in it. And in the Ireland of its time used to having very little, people like Jemmie and Johnny kept the country running.

Michael Lynch is a retired ESB employee from Co Cavan. Married with eight grown-up children, he enjoys writing short stories and poems as a hobby.

AROUND THE FARM GATE

49 Rural Slices

Brigid Daly

THE distant din of the threshing mill coming in the distance.

Playing in the chaff while the neighbouring men tucked in to plates of floury spuds, lashings of creamy butter, bacon and crisp green cabbage.

The sound of the mowing bar and my father's endless whetting of blades.

The grinding noise of the winding of the rope on the hay buggy.

Tea and currant cake in the hay field.

The voice of my mother calling the cows; "Hi Home. Hi Home."

The gushing ting of hand milking into a galvanised bucket.

My mother loading churns of milk on the horse and cart.

The patter of butter in the basin of buttermilk.

The smell of grinding turnips in a mangler for the pigs.

The potato digger tossing potatoes high in the air.

Smoking hay straws in the barn on wet winter Sundays.

Cutting thistles for the sow.

Walking the cow to Bradley's bull three miles away.

Minding a sick calf in the kitchen under the statue of St Brigid.

My father tapping steel shoes onto the mare's hooves.

My father setting off with cattle to the fair of Ballinakill.

Giving the cows extra hay and straw bedding on Christmas Eve.

Washing the doorstep on Christmas Eve.

Frost designs on the inside of the windows in winter.

Travelling in the pony and trap to visit our grandmother.

Our neighbour Andy spending a full day with us in the mid-sixties waiting for the world to end.

The family rosary with all the trimmings.

The smell of crisp white sheets and the brown habit at my grandmothers wake in 1963.

Picking primroses for the May altar.

Travellers calling to the farm to mend tin buckets and selling paper flowers.

The music and set dancing of the American wakes, the night before the yanks returned to America from Shannon.

Pumping the Tilly lamp making sure not to damage the pink mantle.

Picking the colours off the free plastic lampshades supplied with rural electrification in 1957

The first television for the All Ireland final in September 1963.

The buzz of the first milking machine.

Brigid Daly is from Crutt, Castlecomer but now lives on a dairy farm in Kanturk Co Cork. Married with three grown up children and a grandson, she is a retired Assistant Director of Public Health Nursing by profession

50 The Mice In The Meadow

Joe Coyle

YOU tend to remember where you were when you saw your first flying mouse. I was in a field off the N56 in north-west Donegal. The mice certainly flew high that day, but before telling the tale of how they reached for the skies, it's important to know how we got there.

Our family of six had arrived in Gortahork in Easter 1985 after I had spent my first nine years in Glasgow. In the generation before, my father's parents had switched Gortahork for Glasgow in the late 1950s, in search of a bigger town and better living. Off the boat, they lived in the Gorbals for a time, before settling in Annette Street in Govanhill, in the bosom of one of the areas dominated by the Irish in the city.

We lived in Craigie Street, famous for its 'Polis' station and St Bride's School. It took two minutes to walk to school for us, but I didn't like doing it in the shorts my mother insisted I wear. I was a city boy, and city boys don't show their legs. I was five years old.

My mother, a nurse, was also a Donegal evacuee in the big city. And so Sarah from Moville and Michael from Gortahork, like so many others, courted in Glasgow's Irish pubs and clubs – the Claddagh Club was one of their favourite meeting places. After marrying in 1970, they had Donna, Joseph (that's me), Angela and Una.

In October '84, with my parents' mind made up to bring

our family to Ireland after my grandparents on my father's side passed away in the previous years, my Dad took me to my first 'fitba' gem'. But it wasn't Celtic at Parkhead he took me to, but instead to watch Scotland in a World Cup Qualifier against Iceland at Hampden, up the road from our tenement house. He lifted me over the turnstiles that night, not because he was tight with money, but because it was the done thing, and encouraged by the man at the gate. I loved that. Out into the arena; I can still smell the field.

Paul McStay, my absolute hero, scored his first two goals for Scotland that night, one of them a 25-yard screamer, and Charlie Nicholas scored the third in a 3-1 win. Dalglish played too ('C'MON KENNY,' my Dad shouted, every time the King got the ball). Jock Stein was the manager. It may as well have been Celtic playing that night.

So in Easter 1985, I became Irish. I knew how to say *oíche mhaith*, but that was about the height of it. School in Gortahork for a year, then over the road to Falcarragh for the rest of my primary and secondary education.

I was Irish, but I couldn't shake old habits. I entered the Community Games' arts competition and my drawing probably wasn't what the judges expected. I drew Daley Thompson, the black Englishman who the previous year had won decathlon gold for Great Britain in the Los Angeles Olympics, for which I was awarded second prize.

Within months of arriving in Ireland, Dennis Taylor had beaten Steve Davis to win the World Snooker Championship, and Barry McGuigan became champion of the world. Back in Scotland, Celtic were winning nothing as Alex Ferguson's Aberdeen dominated. There was nothing for a boy like me in Glasgow, I thought. It was Donegal, and that was alright with me. Our family had made the right move, after all.

And oh... the freedom. My sisters and I went exploring often, in the fields around our house. And the shore closeby teemed with periwinkles. A big man with a beard from Sligo used to call to pick up the bags of winkles I had collected, and he sold them to the restaurants around the country and on to France, he told us. I was earning big bucks (£12 a bag, and more in the winter) and was able to buy tapes for my ZX Spectrum computer with my own money. I thought I was a grown man when I got paid.

We netted salmon illegally in the middle of the night in the waters behind our house. We ate the fish ourselves, though, and what we didn't eat, we gave to our neighbours, so as far as my Dad and uncles were concerned, there was nothing really illegal about it. We footed turf in the bogs beneath the Derryveagh mountains. I didn't particularly love the bog, but the reward of a Football Special and crisps at the end of a back-breaking day made it all worth it.

It was on that bog road that I, like so many others in my area, learned to drive. I wasn't yet a teenager but if it was quiet on the road late of an evening, my Dad would get into the passenger seat, his way of saying, 'you drive, son'.

I learned how to drive a tractor around that time too. Well, I learned how *not* to drive a tractor. I'm going to blame a dodgy clutch – and the fact that the accelerator was controlled by your hand – for nearly killing both me and the farmer, a friend of my Dad's, who let me sit behind the wheel. I let out the clutch, not slowly as the farmer advised, but as if I'd just stood on a rusty nail. The tractor jolted backwards, and we headed for the four-foot drop to the shoreline behind us. The farmer was quick to spot that I was, in fact, fairly clueless as to what to do next. I ended up with nothing more than a sore ear and a sorer foot as he stood on it in the clamber to seize control of the tractor. Funnily enough, that man never let me behind the wheel again, but many years later I bumped into him on the road to Seville in 2003 as Celtic prepared for the Uefa Cup Final, and we laughed about our near-death experience 17 years or so before that. He had a vague memory of the tractor incident; I'll never forget it.

These things just wouldn't have happened if we stayed in Glasgow. We would have other experiences, sure, but I'm fairly certain none of my Glasgow cousins have ever seen a flying mouse...

◆　　◆　　◆

And so we ended up in a meadow off the N56 in August 1987, a city boy and his father, helping a neighbour and his two young sons to cut the grass. The sun shone and we were making hay; I can still smell the field.

I didn't have a notion what was going on to begin with, but as far as I could make out, it was all great craic. We were getting things done, but it didn't feel like work at all (maybe that's because us young lads played football on the sidelines most of that day).

But we helped, too, following the Massey Ferguson and its 'mowing arm' around and around the field, working in towards the middle from the outer perimeter, collecting the grass, packaging it up, throwing it in heaps. Moving on to the next bit, packaging it up, throwing it in heaps. Playing a bit of football. Moving on to the next bit of grass, packaging it up, throwing it in heaps. Inwards towards the middle of the field, until there was only a nipple of grass left.

As the tractor made the final turn-around and aimed at

the centre of the field, the two young lads were giddy with excitement, with the older of the two swinging his left leg at thin air, as if practising a free kick.

At that moment, I was just thinking: 'Great, we're nearly done...' but as time stood still for a moment, I knew something was afoot. I didn't look at my Dad or the tractor driver. I just wondered why this lad was swinging his leg at thin-air...

And so the tractor's mowing arm moved over the last piece of meadow, and as it did, a swarm of field mice were thrown from behind the tractor. The two lads rushed in with gusto, delighted with themselves, kicking the half-dead mice high into the air. I was in utter shock. After all, I had just seen my first mouse, never mind a flying mouse. And now there were loads of them being kicked in the air half-alive, half-dead and believe me, some were really, really dead.

It was cruel. It was brutal. But it was brilliant.

Joe Coyle is a journalist and designer of newspapers, magazines and books from his office in Gweedore. Born in Glasgow of Irish parents, his family returned to Donegal where he now lives with his wife and three children.

Also From
Ballpoint Press

A Fly Never Lit is the third in a trilogy of memoirs by author PJ
Cunningham about rural life in Ireland from the 1960s and
1970s.

It follows on from *The Lie Of The Land*, which was published
in 2013, and *The Long Acre*, published in 2014, which was
shortlisted for the Bord Gais Energy Irish Book Awards for
Irish Book Of The Year.

A Fly Never Lit examines the characters and events of a
changing Ireland of that time. It is written with the keen
perception of an eye-witness carefully watching and listening
as someone clearly fascinated by the flow of 'ordinary plenty'
in the daily life of rural Ireland.

AROUND THE FARM GATE